Italian Literature: A Very Short Introduction

VERY SHORT INTRODUCTIONS are for anyone wanting a stimulating and accessible way into a new subject. They are written by experts, and have been translated into more than 45 different languages.

The series began in 1995, and now covers a wide variety of topics in every discipline. The VSI library now contains over 500 volumes—a Very Short Introduction to everything from Psychology and Philosophy of Science to American History and Relativity—and continues to grow in every subject area.

Titles in the series include the following:

AFRICAN HISTORY John Parker and
    Richard Rathbone
AGEING Nancy A. Pachana
AGNOSTICISM Robin Le Poidevin
AGRICULTURE Paul Brassley and
    Richard Soffe
ALEXANDER THE GREAT
    Hugh Bowden
ALGEBRA Peter M. Higgins
AMERICAN HISTORY Paul S. Boyer
AMERICAN IMMIGRATION
    David A. Gerber
AMERICAN LEGAL HISTORY
    G. Edward White
AMERICAN POLITICAL
    HISTORY Donald Critchlow
AMERICAN POLITICAL PARTIES
    AND ELECTIONS L. Sandy Maisel
AMERICAN POLITICS
    Richard M. Valelly
THE AMERICAN PRESIDENCY
    Charles O. Jones
AMERICAN SLAVERY
    Heather Andrea Williams
THE AMERICAN WEST Stephen Aron
AMERICAN WOMEN'S HISTORY
    Susan Ware
ANAESTHESIA Aidan O'Donnell
ANARCHISM Colin Ward
ANCIENT EGYPT Ian Shaw
ANCIENT GREECE Paul Cartledge
THE ANCIENT NEAR EAST
    Amanda H. Podany
ANCIENT PHILOSOPHY Julia Annas

ANCIENT WARFARE Harry Sidebottom
ANGLICANISM Mark Chapman
THE ANGLO-SAXON AGE John Blair
ANIMAL BEHAVIOUR
    Tristram D. Wyatt
ANIMAL RIGHTS David DeGrazia
ANXIETY Daniel Freeman and
    Jason Freeman
ARCHAEOLOGY Paul Bahn
ARISTOTLE Jonathan Barnes
ART HISTORY Dana Arnold
ART THEORY Cynthia Freeland
ASTROPHYSICS James Binney
ATHEISM Julian Baggini
THE ATMOSPHERE Paul I. Palmer
AUGUSTINE Henry Chadwick
THE AZTECS David Carrasco
BABYLONIA Trevor Bryce
BACTERIA Sebastian G. B. Amyes
BANKING John Goddard and
    John O. S. Wilson
BARTHES Jonathan Culler
BEAUTY Roger Scruton
THE BIBLE John Riches
BLACK HOLES Katherine Blundell
BLOOD Chris Cooper
THE BODY Chris Shilling
THE BOOK OF MORMON
    Terryl Givens
BORDERS Alexander C. Diener and
    Joshua Hagen
THE BRAIN Michael O'Shea
THE BRICS Andrew F. Cooper
BRITISH POLITICS Anthony Wright

BUDDHA Michael Carrithers
BUDDHISM Damien Keown
BUDDHIST ETHICS Damien Keown
BYZANTIUM Peter Sarris
CANCER Nicholas James
CAPITALISM James Fulcher
CATHOLICISM Gerald O'Collins
CAUSATION Stephen Mumford and
    Rani Lill Anjum
THE CELL Terence Allen and
    Graham Cowling
THE CELTS Barry Cunliffe
CHEMISTRY Peter Atkins
CHILD PSYCHOLOGY Usha Goswami
CHINESE LITERATURE Sabina Knight
CHOICE THEORY Michael Allingham
CHRISTIAN ART Beth Williamson
CHRISTIAN ETHICS D. Stephen Long
CHRISTIANITY Linda Woodhead
CIRCADIAN RHYTHMS Russell Foster
    and Leon Kreitzman
CITIZENSHIP Richard Bellamy
CLASSICAL MYTHOLOGY
    Helen Morales
CLASSICS Mary Beard and
    John Henderson
CLIMATE Mark Maslin
CLIMATE CHANGE Mark Maslin
COGNITIVE NEUROSCIENCE
    Richard Passingham
THE COLD WAR Robert McMahon
COLONIAL AMERICA Alan Taylor
COLONIAL LATIN AMERICAN
    LITERATURE Rolena Adorno
COMBINATORICS Robin Wilson
COMMUNISM Leslie Holmes
COMPLEXITY John H. Holland
THE COMPUTER Darrel Ince
COMPUTER SCIENCE Subrata Dasgupta
CONFUCIANISM Daniel K. Gardner
CONSCIOUSNESS Susan Blackmore
CONTEMPORARY ART
    Julian Stallabrass
CONTEMPORARY FICTION
    Robert Eaglestone
CONTINENTAL PHILOSOPHY
    Simon Critchley
CORAL REEFS Charles Sheppard
CORPORATE SOCIAL
    RESPONSIBILITY Jeremy Moon
COSMOLOGY Peter Coles
CRIMINAL JUSTICE Julian V. Roberts
CRITICAL THEORY
    Stephen Eric Bronner
THE CRUSADES Christopher Tyerman
CRYSTALLOGRAPHY A. M. Glazer
DADA AND SURREALISM
    David Hopkins
DANTE Peter Hainsworth and
    David Robey
DARWIN Jonathan Howard
THE DEAD SEA SCROLLS Timothy Lim
DECOLONIZATION Dane Kennedy
DEMOCRACY Bernard Crick
DEPRESSION Jan Scott and
    Mary Jane Tacchi
DERRIDA Simon Glendinning
DESIGN John Heskett
DEVELOPMENTAL BIOLOGY
    Lewis Wolpert
DIASPORA Kevin Kenny
DINOSAURS David Norman
DREAMING J. Allan Hobson
DRUGS Les Iversen
DRUIDS Barry Cunliffe
THE EARTH Martin Redfern
EARTH SYSTEM SCIENCE Tim Lenton
ECONOMICS Partha Dasgupta
EGYPTIAN MYTH Geraldine Pinch
EIGHTEENTH-CENTURY BRITAIN
    Paul Langford
THE ELEMENTS Philip Ball
EMOTION Dylan Evans
EMPIRE Stephen Howe
ENGLISH LITERATURE Jonathan Bate
THE ENLIGHTENMENT
    John Robertson
ENVIRONMENTAL
    ECONOMICS Stephen Smith
ENVIRONMENTAL
    POLITICS Andrew Dobson
EPICUREANISM Catherine Wilson
EPIDEMIOLOGY Rodolfo Saracci
ETHICS Simon Blackburn
THE ETRUSCANS Christopher Smith
EUGENICS Philippa Levine
THE EUROPEAN UNION John Pinder
    and Simon Usherwood
EVOLUTION Brian and
    Deborah Charlesworth

EXISTENTIALISM Thomas Flynn
THE EYE Michael Land
FAMILY LAW Jonathan Herring
FASCISM Kevin Passmore
FEMINISM Margaret Walters
FILM Michael Wood
FILM MUSIC Kathryn Kalinak
THE FIRST WORLD WAR
    Michael Howard
FOOD John Krebs
FORENSIC PSYCHOLOGY David Canter
FORENSIC SCIENCE Jim Fraser
FORESTS Jaboury Ghazoul
FOSSILS Keith Thomson
FOUCAULT Gary Gutting
FREE SPEECH Nigel Warburton
FREE WILL Thomas Pink
FREUD Anthony Storr
FUNDAMENTALISM Malise Ruthven
FUNGI Nicholas P. Money
THE FUTURE Jennifer M. Gidley
GALAXIES John Gribbin
GALILEO Stillman Drake
GAME THEORY Ken Binmore
GANDHI Bhikhu Parekh
GEOGRAPHY John Matthews and
    David Herbert
GEOPOLITICS Klaus Dodds
GERMAN LITERATURE Nicholas Boyle
GERMAN PHILOSOPHY Andrew Bowie
GLOBAL CATASTROPHES Bill McGuire
GLOBAL ECONOMIC HISTORY
    Robert C. Allen
GLOBALIZATION Manfred Steger
GOD John Bowker
GRAVITY Timothy Clifton
THE GREAT DEPRESSION AND THE
    NEW DEAL Eric Rauchway
HABERMAS James Gordon Finlayson
THE HEBREW BIBLE AS LITERATURE
    Tod Linafelt
HEGEL Peter Singer
HERODOTUS Jennifer T. Roberts
HIEROGLYPHS Penelope Wilson
HINDUISM Kim Knott
HISTORY John H. Arnold
THE HISTORY OF ASTRONOMY
    Michael Hoskin
THE HISTORY OF CHEMISTRY
    William H. Brock

THE HISTORY OF LIFE
    Michael Benton
THE HISTORY OF MATHEMATICS
    Jacqueline Stedall
THE HISTORY OF MEDICINE
    William Bynum
THE HISTORY OF TIME
    Leofranc Holford-Strevens
HIV AND AIDS Alan Whiteside
HOLLYWOOD Peter Decherney
HUMAN ANATOMY
    Leslie Klenerman
HUMAN EVOLUTION Bernard Wood
HUMAN RIGHTS Andrew Clapham
THE ICE AGE Jamie Woodward
IDEOLOGY Michael Freeden
INDIAN PHILOSOPHY Sue Hamilton
THE INDUSTRIAL REVOLUTION
    Robert C. Allen
INFECTIOUS DISEASE Marta L. Wayne
    and Benjamin M. Bolker
INFINITY Ian Stewart
INFORMATION Luciano Floridi
INNOVATION Mark Dodgson and
    David Gann
INTELLIGENCE Ian J. Deary
INTERNATIONAL
    MIGRATION Khalid Koser
INTERNATIONAL RELATIONS
    Paul Wilkinson
IRAN Ali M. Ansari
ISLAM Malise Ruthven
ISLAMIC HISTORY Adam Silverstein
ISOTOPES Rob Ellam
ITALIAN LITERATURE
    Peter Hainsworth and David Robey
JESUS Richard Bauckham
JOURNALISM Ian Hargreaves
JUDAISM Norman Solomon
JUNG Anthony Stevens
KABBALAH Joseph Dan
KANT Roger Scruton
KNOWLEDGE Jennifer Nagel
THE KORAN Michael Cook
LATE ANTIQUITY Gillian Clark
LAW Raymond Wacks
THE LAWS OF THERMODYNAMICS
    Peter Atkins
LEADERSHIP Keith Grint
LEARNING Mark Haselgrove

LEIBNIZ Maria Rosa Antognazza
LIBERALISM Michael Freeden
LIGHT Ian Walmsley
LINGUISTICS Peter Matthews
LITERARY THEORY Jonathan Culler
LOCKE John Dunn
LOGIC Graham Priest
MACHIAVELLI Quentin Skinner
MAGIC Owen Davies
MAGNA CARTA Nicholas Vincent
MAGNETISM Stephen Blundell
MARINE BIOLOGY Philip V. Mladenov
MARTIN LUTHER Scott H. Hendrix
MARTYRDOM Jolyon Mitchell
MARX Peter Singer
MATERIALS Christopher Hall
MATHEMATICS Timothy Gowers
THE MEANING OF LIFE
    Terry Eagleton
MEASUREMENT David Hand
MEDICAL ETHICS Tony Hope
MEDIEVAL BRITAIN John Gillingham
    and Ralph A. Griffiths
MEDIEVAL LITERATURE
    Elaine Treharne
MEDIEVAL PHILOSOPHY
    John Marenbon
MEMORY Jonathan K. Foster
METAPHYSICS Stephen Mumford
MICROBIOLOGY Nicholas P. Money
MICROECONOMICS Avinash Dixit
MICROSCOPY Terence Allen
THE MIDDLE AGES Miri Rubin
MILITARY JUSTICE Eugene R. Fidell
MINERALS David Vaughan
MODERN ART David Cottington
MODERN CHINA Rana Mitter
MODERN FRANCE
    Vanessa R. Schwartz
MODERN IRELAND Senia Pašeta
MODERN ITALY Anna Cento Bull
MODERN JAPAN
    Christopher Goto-Jones
MODERNISM Christopher Butler
MOLECULAR BIOLOGY Aysha Divan
    and Janice A. Royds
MOLECULES Philip Ball
MOONS David A. Rothery
MOUNTAINS Martin F. Price
MUHAMMAD Jonathan A. C. Brown

MUSIC Nicholas Cook
MYTH Robert A. Segal
THE NAPOLEONIC WARS
    Mike Rapport
NELSON MANDELA Elleke Boehmer
NEOLIBERALISM Manfred Steger and
    Ravi Roy
NEWTON Robert Iliffe
NIETZSCHE Michael Tanner
NINETEENTH-CENTURY BRITAIN
    Christopher Harvie and
    H. C. G. Matthew
NORTH AMERICAN INDIANS
    Theda Perdue and Michael D. Green
NORTHERN IRELAND
    Marc Mulholland
NOTHING Frank Close
NUCLEAR PHYSICS Frank Close
NUMBERS Peter M. Higgins
NUTRITION David A. Bender
THE OLD TESTAMENT
    Michael D. Coogan
ORGANIC CHEMISTRY
    Graham Patrick
THE PALESTINIAN-ISRAELI
    CONFLICT Martin Bunton
PANDEMICS Christian W. McMillen
PARTICLE PHYSICS Frank Close
THE PERIODIC TABLE Eric R. Scerri
PHILOSOPHY Edward Craig
PHILOSOPHY IN THE ISLAMIC
    WORLD Peter Adamson
PHILOSOPHY OF LAW
    Raymond Wacks
PHILOSOPHY OF SCIENCE
    Samir Okasha
PHOTOGRAPHY Steve Edwards
PHYSICAL CHEMISTRY Peter Atkins
PILGRIMAGE Ian Reader
PLAGUE Paul Slack
PLANETS David A. Rothery
PLANTS Timothy Walker
PLATE TECTONICS Peter Molnar
PLATO Julia Annas
POLITICAL PHILOSOPHY
    David Miller
POLITICS Kenneth Minogue
POPULISM Cas Mudde and
    Cristóbal Rovira Kaltwasser
POSTCOLONIALISM Robert Young

POSTMODERNISM Christopher Butler
POSTSTRUCTURALISM
    Catherine Belsey
PREHISTORY Chris Gosden
PRESOCRATIC PHILOSOPHY
    Catherine Osborne
PRIVACY Raymond Wacks
PSYCHIATRY Tom Burns
PSYCHOLOGY Gillian Butler and
    Freda McManus
PSYCHOTHERAPY Tom Burns and
    Eva Burns-Lundgren
PUBLIC ADMINISTRATION
    Stella Z. Theodoulou and Ravi K. Roy
PUBLIC HEALTH Virginia Berridge
QUANTUM THEORY
    John Polkinghorne
RACISM Ali Rattansi
REALITY Jan Westerhoff
THE REFORMATION Peter Marshall
RELATIVITY Russell Stannard
RELIGION IN AMERICA Timothy Beal
THE RENAISSANCE Jerry Brotton
RENAISSANCE ART
    Geraldine A. Johnson
REVOLUTIONS Jack A. Goldstone
RHETORIC Richard Toye
RISK Baruch Fischhoff and John Kadvany
RITUAL Barry Stephenson
RIVERS Nick Middleton
ROBOTICS Alan Winfield
ROMAN BRITAIN Peter Salway
THE ROMAN EMPIRE Christopher Kelly
THE ROMAN REPUBLIC
    David M. Gwynn
RUSSIAN HISTORY Geoffrey Hosking
RUSSIAN LITERATURE Catriona Kelly
THE RUSSIAN REVOLUTION
    S. A. Smith
SAVANNAS Peter A. Furley
SCHIZOPHRENIA Chris Frith and
    Eve Johnstone
SCIENCE AND RELIGION
    Thomas Dixon
THE SCIENTIFIC REVOLUTION
    Lawrence M. Principe
SCOTLAND Rab Houston
SEXUALITY Véronique Mottier
SHAKESPEARE'S COMEDIES Bart van Es

SIKHISM Eleanor Nesbitt
SLEEP Steven W. Lockley and
    Russell G. Foster
SOCIAL AND CULTURAL
    ANTHROPOLOGY
    John Monaghan and Peter Just
SOCIAL PSYCHOLOGY Richard J. Crisp
SOCIAL WORK Sally Holland and
    Jonathan Scourfield
SOCIALISM Michael Newman
SOCIOLOGY Steve Bruce
SOCRATES C. C. W. Taylor
SOUND Mike Goldsmith
THE SOVIET UNION Stephen Lovell
THE SPANISH CIVIL WAR
    Helen Graham
SPANISH LITERATURE Jo Labanyi
SPORT Mike Cronin
STARS Andrew King
STATISTICS David J. Hand
STUART BRITAIN John Morrill
SYMMETRY Ian Stewart
TAXATION Stephen Smith
TELESCOPES Geoff Cottrell
TERRORISM Charles Townshend
THEOLOGY David F. Ford
TIBETAN BUDDHISM
    Matthew T. Kapstein
THE TROJAN WAR Eric H. Cline
THE TUDORS John Guy
TWENTIETH-CENTURY BRITAIN
    Kenneth O. Morgan
THE UNITED NATIONS
    Jussi M. Hanhimäki
THE U.S. CONGRESS Donald A. Ritchie
THE U.S. SUPREME COURT
    Linda Greenhouse
THE VIKINGS Julian Richards
VIRUSES Dorothy H. Crawford
VOLTAIRE Nicholas Cronk
WAR AND TECHNOLOGY
    Alex Roland
WATER John Finney
WILLIAM SHAKESPEARE
    Stanley Wells
WITCHCRAFT Malcolm Gaskill
THE WORLD TRADE
    ORGANIZATION Amrita Narlikar
WORLD WAR II Gerhard L. Weinberg

Peter Hainsworth and David Robey

ITALIAN LITERATURE

A Very Short Introduction

OXFORD
UNIVERSITY PRESS

OXFORD

UNIVERSITY PRESS

Great Clarendon Street, Oxford ox2 6DP

Oxford University Press is a department of the University of Oxford.
It furthers the University's objective of excellence in research, scholarship,
and education by publishing worldwide in

Oxford New York

Auckland Cape Town Dar es Salaam Hong Kong Karachi
Kuala Lumpur Madrid Melbourne Mexico City Nairobi
New Delhi Shanghai Taipei Toronto

With offices in

Argentina Austria Brazil Chile Czech Republic France Greece
Guatemala Hungary Italy Japan Poland Portugal Singapore
South Korea Switzerland Thailand Turkey Ukraine Vietnam

Oxford is a registered trade mark of Oxford University Press
in the UK and in certain other countries

Published in the United States
by Oxford University Press Inc., New York

© Peter Hainsworth and David Robey 2012

The moral rights of the authors have been asserted
Database right Oxford University Press (maker)

First published 2012

British Library Cataloguing in Publication Data

Data available

Library of Congress Cataloging in Publication Data

Library of Congress Control Number: 2012930320

Typeset by SPI Publisher Services, Pondicherry, India
Printed and bound by CPI Group (UK) Ltd, Croydon, CR0 4YY

ISBN 978-0-19-923179-9

Contents

Preface xi

List of illustrations xiii

Introduction 1

1 History 5

2 Tradition 22

3 Theory 44

4 Politics 60

5 Secularism 81

6 Women 99

Further reading 113

Appendix: writers cited 117

Index 121

Preface

The present book follows on from our *Oxford Companion to Italian Literature*, and we owe much to the excellent work of its many contributors. We are also deeply indebted to the comments on an earlier draft from our friends and colleagues Robert Gordon, Martin McLaughlin, and the late and sadly missed Simon Price.

Translations from Italian are our own. The title given in English after the first mention of the Italian title is usually a literal version of the Italian, though we also mention a published English title if this departs radically from the original.

Dates of all authors mentioned are given in the Appendix.

List of illustrations

1   Map of contemporary Italy **xiv**

2   Ferrara: Corso Ercole
    I d'Este **7**
    © Herbert Ortner

3   Ferruccio Vecchi, *The
    Empire Leaping from the
    Head of Mussolini* **17**
    From *La Rivista illustrata del Popolo
    d'Italia*, July 1939, Year XVII

4   Ungaretti at the front in 1916 **23**

5   Giorgio Vasari, *Six Tuscan
    Poets* **32**
    By kind permission of the Provost
    and Fellows of Oriel College, Oxford

6   Italian poets react to Edoardo
    Sanguineti's avant-garde
    poems **38**
    Artist unknown. By permission of
    Siena University

7   Nicolas Poussin, *Rinaldo and
    Armida* **46**
    © Dulwich Picture Gallery, London/
    Bridgeman Art Library

8   Elio Vittorini (right) with
    Alberto Moravia in the
    1950s **61**
    © Farabolafoto

9   Dante and the simoniac
    Popes **67**
    © Biblioteca Nazionale Marciana,
    Venice/Gianni Dagli Orti/The Art
    Archive

10 Italo Svevo smoking **82**
    © Commune di Trieste/Museo
    Sveviano

11 Raphael's portrait of
    Castiglione **91**
    © Europe/Alamy

12 Giovanni Battista Tiepolo,
    *Angelica Coming to the Aid of
    the Wounded Medoro* **93**
    © Villa Valmarana ai Nani, Vicenza/
    Luca Sassi/The Bridgeman Art Library

13 Michelangelo, drawing
    of Vittoria Colonna **107**
    © The British Museum, London/The
    Bridgeman Art Library

1. Map of contemporary Italy

Introduction

There are lots of ways at looking at the literature of a particular country, and some literatures are more difficult to get a perspective on than others. Depending on your point of view, English literature may or may not extend into America, Australia, Scotland, or India, and looking back in time may or may not include Anglo-Saxon. In comparison the Italian case seems unusually straightforward. First, almost all Italian literature has been produced in the peninsula extending from the mountains bordering what is now France, Switzerland, and Austria in the north, down to its farthest southern tip and including Sicily and Sardinia. In spite of massive emigration, little has been written in Italian by people of Italian origin in the Americas and elsewhere, and Italy's short-lived colonies have left almost no post-colonial literary heritage. Secondly, much of the language stays the same over time. The most famous line of verse in Italian is 'Nel mezzo del camin di nostra vita', 'In the middle of the path of our life', the opening line of the *Divine Comedy* written by the Florentine Dante Alighieri in the first decade of the 14th century. Every word is still there in modern Italian, spoken as well as written. Dante's language, like his thought, has many unfamiliar features, but the basic texture is recognizable to the average Italian secondary-school student. Not only that, but there is a broad consensus about who the great authors are, Italian literature's canon of major writers (*maggiori*), from Dante, Petrarch, and Boccaccio, the 'three crowns' (*tre corone*) of the 14th century as Italians call them, through to Giacomo Leopardi and Alessandro Manzoni in the 19th. We would expect more dispute about who qualifies as a modern master, and disputes there have been; but certain names have their places in the canon assured, from Giovanni Verga, Italy's leading realist novelist, in the late 19th century, to Eugenio Montale, who produced some of the best poetry to be written in Europe in the century that followed.

The straightforwardness is of course something of an illusion. The consensus about Italian literature has its origins in the 19th-century Risorgimento, the movement that led to national unification, and in particular in the work of the critic and educationalist Francesco De Sanctis, who saw a national literary tradition as an essential cultural foundation for the new Italian state, and constructed one accordingly in his influential and still widely read history of Italian literature of 1870–1. In spite of, or perhaps because of, the tumultuous developments in the country over the next hundred years, the consensus he established proved remarkably durable, inside and outside Italy. It has of course evolved and adapted, and in the last few decades, following the general trend of academic literary studies, it has come to be seriously questioned. De Sanctis underestimated the whole period from 1600 to 1800, when the country was under foreign rule and, as he saw it, its literature was correspondingly subservient. It would now be absurd to see it simply in that light. At the same time, it has become much harder to separate Italian literature of the Middle Ages and Renaissance from Latin. Up to at least 1600, all the main writers in Italian knew and drew upon classical Latin literature and they also wrote in Latin, in Petrarch's by no means unique case far more than in Italian. Other major areas have emerged from the margins to which they had generally been consigned, notably vernacular literature in the 15th century, dialect literature, and women's writing.

It might seem to follow that the traditional consensus on Italian literature has had its day. While taking account of its imperfections and of the ways in which it is changing, however, we shall be keeping it firmly before us in this book, for a number of reasons. It still tends to dominate the teaching of Italian literature inside and outside Italy, partly because without it Italian literature has no manageable frame or historical shape: so far as we can tell, alternative views (such as they are) presuppose the established canon of major writers rather than beginning again from scratch. In any case, the problem is what the canon is judged to leave out, not what it includes: re-evaluation has led to additions, but not generally to demotions. More importantly for our purposes, the canonical authors are those that a reader with little or no experience of Italian is likely to want to know about – the ones who are most highly thought of in Italy itself, and who have often been large presences on the European or world stage. More importantly still, from our point of view as writers of this book, the authors we talk about are the ones whom we personally think are most significant, and whose work we have most enjoyed reading, studying, and teaching throughout our careers.

Our *Very Short Introduction* is just that, not a short history. Chapters take account of chronology, but they do not adhere to strict historical sequence. Instead they are framed as general discussions of problematic trends and issues that mark out writing in Italian almost from its beginnings. Within these discussions, we focus on particular, generally canonical, authors and texts, not trying to fit them into rigid patterns, but using the broader topics as ways of exploring the individual features that we find most compelling about them, and which we think have had most significance historically and for the modern reader. In our last chapter, on women as figures written about and as authors in their own right, we depart most from the traditional consensus to deal with one of the issues which until recently was marginalized in

Italy itself, but which readers outside the country find especially arresting. We are not of course trying to say everything there is to say about this or any other of the authors and topics we discuss, but rather to open up avenues that readers will find interesting to follow, and, we hope, eventually depart from on independent explorations of their own.

Chapter 1
History

Il caro, il dolce, il pio passato

[The dear, the sweet, the blessed past]
(Bassani)

Towards the beginning of *Il giardino dei Finzi-Contini* (*The Garden of the Finzi-Continis*), published in 1962, Giorgio Bassani describes the location of the garden that gives his novel its title, a magnificent, vast, ancient park on the edge of the city of Ferrara, with at its centre the Finzi-Continis' Neo-Gothic mansion. The park and the mansion are imaginary, but the location is geographically precise, next to the Renaissance city walls at the end of Ferrara's most famous Renaissance street, Corso Ercole I d'Este. Here is Bassani's description:

> Immortalized by Giosuè Carducci and Gabriele D'Annunzio, this Ferrara street is so familiar to lovers of art and poetry world-wide that any description of it would only be superfluous. As is well known, it is at the very heart of that Northern part of the city which was added in the Renaissance to the cramped medieval township, and which for that very reason is called the *Addizione Erculea*. Broad, running straight as a sword from the Castello to the Mura degli Angeli, flanked for its entire length by the dark mass of aristocratic dwellings, with its distant, sublime background of red

brick, green vegetation and sky that truly seems to lead you to the infinite: Corso Ercole I d'Este is so handsome, such is its appeal to tourists, that the joint Socialist-Communist administration that has governed Ferrara for more than fifteen years has recognized the need to leave it untouched, to defend it with the utmost rigour against any new building or shopping development, in short to conserve whole its original aristocratic character.

The reader, it is implicitly assumed, will be among the 'lovers of art and poetry world-wide' who have admired the street in person or read the celebrations of it in verse by Carducci and D'Annunzio, two poets who in very different ways gave voice to the aspirations of the newly united Italy that came into being in 1870. But much of the street's appeal comes, in Bassani's description, from its older history and the history of Ferrara. It is named after the 15th-century ruler, Ercole I d'Este, who built onto the old city the 'addition' that is also named after him, giving the present *centro storico* the form that it still has, and marking the high point of Ferrara's urban development for half a millennium to come. The fact that the street has survived intact, Bassani points out, is largely due to the efforts of the post-war city administration to preserve it against modernizing commercial interests. The administration is itself a coalition of Communists and Socialists, both of whom had had revolutionary programmes in the past, but by the 1960s were part of Italy's democratic system. In Ferrara, as in many other cities, they kept up mildly social-democratic initiatives of various sorts, including the defence of Italy's historical heritage against the entrepreneurial capitalism that created the so-called economic miracle of the late 1950s and early 1960s.

Bassani called his collected novels and stories the 'Novel of Ferrara', and in a sense the city is what they are about. They mostly focus on Ferrara's Jewish community, of which Bassani himself was part, from the 1920s to the deportation of the great majority of its members to Auschwitz in November 1943, from

2. Ferrara: Corso Ercole I d'Este. The Este castle is in the background. Bassani sets the Finzi-Contini garden at the opposite end

where almost none returned. The impending calamity haunts *Il giardino dei Finzi-Contini*, by far his richest and most affecting novel, which evokes the strange, almost idyllic calm, embodied in the garden of the title, of middle- and upper-class Jewish life in the pre-war years, in the face of the increasing anti-Semitism of Mussolini's regime and the growing awareness that a dreadful war and worse are inevitable. The narrator is a fictionalized version of the author, and at the centre of his youthful world is his unhappy love for the spirited, elusive Micòl, the daughter of the Finzi-Contini family, who tries to cancel out the future by living only in the present or the past. Micòl's deportation and death are only briefly mentioned, and we are not told how the narrator survived. But throughout the novel what is not said or only alluded to is as important as the detailed evocation of 1930s Ferrara which the narrator lovingly and movingly gives us.

There is an interplay here between deeply personal memories, the history of a city, national politics, and the tragedy of the Jews of Europe. By no means all Italian literature has such complex and far-reaching resonances, nor does it all evoke the past so explicitly and directly; but in one way or another, much of it bears the imprint of a particular place, and none of it can be understood without some knowledge of the peculiar course of Italian history. The phrase which we have put at the head of this chapter, Micòl's poignant but gently ironic reference to 'The dear, the sweet, the blessed past', not only expresses her personal desperation, but can also stand for much that is interesting and distinctive about Italian literature as a whole.

* * *

Like other cities in central and northern Italy, Ferrara has a very long tradition of civic independence, which at various times has meant political independence as well. A network of municipalities had remained after the disintegration of the Roman Empire in the 5th and 6th centuries AD; nearby Bologna was one. Others, including Ferrara, came into being in the early Middle Ages, taking on some of the features of the old Roman urban culture preserved elsewhere. This substantial continuity of urban life from the classical world into the Middle Ages marks a major difference between Italy and northern Europe. It was the condition for the remarkable growth in trade, agriculture, and manufacture that occurred in the northern and central Italian regions from the 11th century and earlier, leading the economic revival that took place north of the Alps during the centuries that followed. By the 12th century, Ferrara was one of a large number of prosperous self-governing communes, miniature republics controlled by the principal families of the city, each with its imposing cathedral and civic buildings. It was a world in which the countryside was dominated by the towns, in contrast to countries further north. By the end of the 13th century, the largest cities in Europe after Paris were probably Florence, Venice, Milan, and Genoa; Florence, the birthplace of modern banking, was the richest of all; London was considerably smaller.

The economic growth of the communes suffered a severe setback with the Black Death of 1348, which halved the population of the larger cities. Major political changes were also taking place. The world of the communes was one of endemic conflict, most famously between Guelphs, the party of the Pope, and Ghibellines, the party of the Holy Roman Emperor, and this was the main reason for the communes' end. The territorial expansion of a few states subordinated most into larger units, and at the same time republicanism gave way, as a result of factional strife, to rule by single lords, *signorie*, which then developed into hereditary dynasties with courts. In the later 13th century, Ferrara was fought over by the Este and Torelli families; the Este won and remained in power until the end of the 16th century, expanding the boundaries of their state, and assuming the title of Dukes in 1471. This was the period of the city's glory. The Este not only brought about the elegant urban expansion to which Bassani refers, but also made their court one of the leading cultural centres of Italy and of all Europe. It played a major role in the development of humanism, the revived study of the language, history, and culture of ancient Greece and Rome, which became the driving force behind the cultural rebirth for which the term 'Renaissance' stands. In the 15th century, Ferrara hosted the famous humanist school of Guarino da Verona, where the Este princes were taught, and in the 16th century it was a leading centre for painting, music, and vernacular literature. Three of the greatest Renaissance narrative poets, Matteo Maria Boiardo, Ludovico Ariosto, and Torquato Tasso, lived within the ambit of the Este court and wrote for it in the first instance.

Traditionally dated 1400–1600 by Italian historians, the Renaissance was divided by an event that had profound political and cultural consequences, making the preceding decades of intermittent internal warfare seem more like a period of peace. In 1494, the French invaded, causing Boiardo to break off his rollicking epic, the *Orlando innamorato* (*Orlando in Love*), long before he had tied all the narrative threads together. Soon after came the Spanish. The traumatic wars which followed culminated in the Sack of Rome in 1527. Deeply involved in this conflict, and repeatedly at risk of annexation by the Papacy, Ferrara managed to survive as an independent duchy until the death of the last Duke in 1597. It then came under Papal control and remained part of the so-called Papal States until national unification in 1861. By then, it had long assumed a modest provincial status, remaining physically more or less intact within the Renaissance walls to which Bassani refers. Following the slow pace of economic and social progress in Italy, which left Ferrara, like many other Italian cities, relatively unchanged during the 19th century, the extensive farmland within the walls survived until after World War II. The cathedral, the medieval communal buildings, and, most notably, the massive Este castle surrounded by its moat, all continue to dominate the city centre today.

Ferrara's trajectory is similar to that of Milan, Parma, Mantua, and many other cities of central and northern Italy, which fell under Spanish or Papal rule by the end of the 16th century. Genoa survived as an independent republic until the rising kingdom of Piedmont-Savoy absorbed it in the mid-18th century, laying with this expansion the foundations for the kingdom's future role in the unified Italian state. Only the Republic of Venice and the Grand Duchy of Tuscany, which had absorbed the old republic of Florence, survived as independent states until the Napoleonic period. The south is a different story. Naples and Sicily were ruled, mostly together, by a succession of European royal houses, beginning with the Normans in the 11th century. Urban and economic development was limited, and the feudal nobility retained dominance until well after the Renaissance, often with unenlightened ruthlessness. It is not easy to say exactly where the south begins, and it has never been a homogeneous unity; but the north–south split was and is a real one, with immense consequences for every aspect of Italian life, not least Italian literature.

At the end of the 18th century, most of the peninsula was under foreign domination, the dominant power now having become Austria. The French Revolution at first offered new hopes to the small number of patriots who dreamed of a renewed united Italy, but the Risorgimento, the movement of unification, was not successful for several tumultuous decades. When Napoleon invaded in 1796, he established two Italian republics across the north and centre of the peninsula, but these and most of the rest of the country stayed directly or indirectly under French control. After Napoleon's fall, Italy's 18th-century boundaries were largely restored, Austria increased its dominance, and the movement for liberation was severely repressed; leading figures, such as the republican theorist and activist Giuseppe Mazzini and the romantic revolutionary Giuseppe Garibaldi, spent years in exile. Yet the momentum gradually increased, and unification eventually took place surprisingly quickly. In 1860, Garibaldi and his thousand followers landed in Sicily, while in the north the Piedmontese army inflicted a series of bloody defeats on the Austrians. By the end of the year, Victor Emanuel II of Piedmont was King of Italy, though the Veneto remained under Austrian rule for almost another six years, and the Papacy retained power in the centre until the troops of the new kingdom finally stormed Rome in 1870, leaving the Pope with nothing but the present Vatican City.

* * *

This long history of division and foreign domination had a number of important consequences for Italian literature, the most fundamental of which concerns language. Indeed the remarkable thing is that a national language and literature came into being at all. Actually the literature came first and a language was built out of it. Dante, Petrarch, and Boccaccio, the 'three crowns', created works of literature in the 14th century which were recognized as comparable to the great works of antiquity, in Dante's case almost immediately. All three were Tuscans and the language they wrote in was grounded in Tuscan usage, in important respects specifically in the usage of Florence, which was Dante's native city, the city of Petrarch's family, and the city controlling the small town of Certaldo where Boccaccio was born. But none of their writing was purely Tuscan or Florentine, just as their thought, reading, and imagination were anything but provincial. Before they died, or very soon after, all three were already being imitated in one way or another by authors from outside Tuscany. From then, they would be by turns admired, pilloried, debated, imitated, and parodied, but would remain ineradicable reference points for any serious writing in any form of Italian vernacular. The rules for imitating their language would be formulated with great precision in the 16th century, and after that Italian existed as a national literary language, although debates about the nature of that language, the *questione della lingua*, continued well into the 19th century and beyond. Even then, Italian was spoken only by a small elite, and its characteristic rhetoric was forbidding. Italy's greatest 19th-century novelist Alessandro Manzoni, a Milanese who grew up more comfortable speaking French than Italian, reshaped literary Italian and the Italian novel in his *Promessi sposi* (*The Betrothed*), the final version of which was published in 1840. Yet it would be more than a century before novelists could write Italian with any immediacy. The Triestine novelist Svevo observed in his *La coscienza di Zeno* (*Zeno's Conscience*, also *The Confessions of Zeno*) of 1923 that 'with every Tuscan word we write we tell a lie'; and ten years later, in the preface to his first novel, *Fontamara*, Ignazio Silone wrote that for people from the Abruzzo like himself learning Italian was like learning Latin.

All this is because in Italy, as a result of the centuries of political disunity, the position of dialects in relation to the national language has been quite different from the corresponding position in Britain or France. These dialects are independent developments

12

from the spoken Latin of the Roman Empire, and remained the normal spoken language of most Italians of all classes until quite late in the 20th century, in spite of Unification. Only by the 1990s, largely under the impact of television, had Italian become the language spoken on a day-to-day basis by the great majority of the population, as flexible and immediate as most other contemporary European languages, with fads, slang, English and American imports, and regional and class variations. But predominantly dialect-speaking areas remain, and there are still strong traces of the old dialects in popular speech. We shall explore further in the chapters that follow ways in which the peculiar historical relationship between *lingua* (the Italian language) and *dialetto* has conditioned the whole course of Italian literature.

The broad political trajectory we have outlined, from communes to regional courts to foreign domination to national liberation and Unification, also helps to explain some of the general features of Italian literature at the different stages of its development: quite socially diverse in the Middle Ages, aristocratic in the Renaissance, relatively stagnant in the 17th and 18th centuries, dominated by Risorgimento politics in the 19th. But disunity had further, more fundamental, and persistent consequences. Most obviously, the absence of a national capital from the fall of the Roman Empire until Unification has given Italian literature a strongly regional character. In France and Britain, the development of the nation state from the Renaissance onwards meant that society and culture were increasingly dominated by the capital city, which was the source and regulator of the national language as well. Before Unification, Rome's symbolic and ecclesiastical importance meant that it played a major part in Italian politics, without ever becoming the main centre of political or economic power. It was a major artistic and cultural centre during the Renaissance, but not as important for literature as it was for art and architecture. When it again became a magnet for writers after Unification, it was by no means able to assert unquestioned literary primacy. To a large extent, that is still the case today.

The history of Italian literature is thus in large part the history of the different regional centres in which it developed. It had its beginnings in the first half of the 13th century with a group of poet officials at the rich and diverse Sicilian court of the German Emperor Frederick II, spreading from there to the merchant communes of north and central Italy. The connection with Dante, Petrarch, and Boccaccio gave Florence its enduring literary and linguistic prestige. In the later 15th century, under the rule of Lorenzo de' Medici, it became the major centre of literary and intellectual activity in the whole of Italy, but not for long: as we have seen, in the 16th century Ferrara was one of the leading cultural centres in Europe. Much later, in the 1860s, Florence was the provisional national capital until Rome was taken in 1870, and became once again the city to which writers and intellectuals tended to gravitate: for several decades, the Giubbe rosse café in Piazza Repubblica was the rendezvous of choice for the country's impoverished but sophisticated literary elite. But after the end of World War II, the major literary centres were the two economic powerhouses, Milan and Turin. Milan had a strong tradition of dialect literature going back to the Middle Ages, and had been the home city of some of the most important intellectuals and writers from the 18th century, as well as the major centre of Italian Romanticism and its successors. Now it became the home of the country's greatest modern poet, Eugenio Montale, who moved there from Florence to work as a journalist for the *Corriere della sera*. At the same time, a hundred kilometres away in Turin, Italo Calvino, Cesare Pavese, and Natalia Ginzburg were making their employer Einaudi the most exciting publisher in Italy, and producing some of their best work.

In the south, Naples became a centre of French culture in the 14th century, and would remain a focus for literary and intellectual activity for centuries to come, while the south as a whole went into prolonged cultural as well as economic decline. It was not just the peasants who left Sicily looking for a better life elsewhere, but many of the island's (and subsequently the country's) most important authors, including Giovanni Verga, the leading figure of Italian 19th-century naturalism, who went to Florence and then Milan, and the country's most famous modern playwright, Luigi Pirandello, who lived most of his life in Rome. Over the centuries, many other Italian writers have sought patronage or refuge away from their home cities. Dante is the exemplary case. Exiled from Florence, when his White Guelph party was ousted by the Blacks in 1301, he spent the rest of his life in various northern Italian courts, bitterly resentful of the enemies and the city that had forced him out. Petrarch, whose father was exiled in the same wave as Dante, spent his life on the move, living only a few years in one place or another, first in Provence and then in northern Italy, 'an exile everywhere', as he put it.

* * *

We have so far jumped over the most troubling period in modern Italian history. From 1921 until 1943, Italy was a Fascist state, headed by a leader, Benito Mussolini, who came to power legitimately and enjoyed massive public support for at least fifteen years, but whose policies eventually led to military defeat, civil war, collaboration in the Nazi genocide, and his own violent death. Even today, the trauma of World War II has not completely healed, and marks almost all the writing of the post-war period until well into the 1980s.

Fascism came about as a result of the crises and failures that followed on Unification in 1870. As many a realist novelist testified, the geographical and social divisions within the country remained as they were before, and for many people, particularly the southern peasantry, conditions became worse. Governments tried to show their strength by colonial adventures in North Africa and repressive measures at home, but they were repeatedly seen as feeble, directionless, and corrupt. This climate did not augur well for parliamentary democracy, which in any case rested on a minority electorate. The great majority of the population were peasants, dialect-speaking and mostly illiterate. Compared to northern Europe, the economy was backward, though industrial development accelerated in the north from the beginning of the 20th century. The small middle class contained most supporters of the Risorgimento, but also a high proportion of practising Catholics who were sensitive to the condemnation of the new state by the politically dispossessed Papacy. By the early 20th century, the growth of revolutionary socialism on the left and increasingly violent nationalism on the right were making the political system and the country increasingly unstable.

Italy entered World War I on the side of Britain and France in 1915 and emerged on the winning side, but the benefits were negligible. With the economy in crisis, unemployment rampant, militant socialism and communism apparently in the ascendant, the Fascists were able to present themselves as a party of strength and order which was both revolutionary and the successor to the Risorgimento tradition. Fascist totalitarianism seemed to bring relative prosperity, domestic peace, and the healing of conflicts, particularly when, in 1929, Mussolini resolved the division between Church and State by signing the Concordat with the Vatican. Nor did the political constraints seem all that oppressive: individuals had a broad freedom of manoeuvre to write and say what they wanted, even in the area of politics, so long as the Duce and Fascism itself were not called into question. Montale, who was always sceptical about Mussolini and later became a resolute anti-Fascist, was not alone in looking back to the years between the wars as a time of civilized and cultured ease.

Despite some disturbing shifts of policy in the later 1930s, real opposition remained negligible, particularly from intellectuals and writers, other than those in exile. The end, when it came, was through war. Italy entered World War II on Hitler's side in 1940, and fought for the most part disastrously. When the Allies invaded Sicily in 1943, Mussolini's support collapsed and he was voted out of government, only to be reinstated by the Germans as head of a

3. Ferruccio Vecchi, *The Empire Leaping from the Head of Mussolini*. A striking variation on the modernism characteristic of much Fascist art

puppet Republic based in the small town of Salò on Lake Garda. This was when Mussolini's anti-Semitic policies became a Nazi-led programme of systematic deportation to the death camps, and for the first time an effective opposition emerged, in the form of a largely Communist-led resistance which fought a partisan campaign against the *repubblichini* of Salò in the centre and north. When the war ended in 1945, it could thus be reasonably claimed that Italy had been on the side of the victors for two important years.

Bassani's novel looks back on the late 1930s from the perspective of the early 1960s. The post-war Italian state had been founded on the anti-Fascist ideals of the Resistance, but by then disillusion and conflict had again set in. The problem was that not much seemed to have changed. The bureaucracy, judiciary, and police force were substantially continuous with those of the Fascist period. The Christian Democrats, who dominated government from 1948 until 1992, were dedicated to the support of the Catholic Church, opposition to Communism, and the preservation of the status quo and the client network on which the system depended; the inclusion of the moderate socialists in their coalitions did little to change the direction of government. The Communists provided the main opposition party after 1948, and remained excluded from national government, in spite of increasingly distancing themselves from the Soviet Union and retaining strong electoral support – though, as in Bassani's Ferrara, they played a major role in local administrations. In a climate of general lack of faith in the state and its government, writers and intellectuals tended to align themselves with one form or another of the political left. But while the worker and student movements of 1968 brought a brief hope of radical change, no such thing occurred. The next decade was marked by terrorism from both left and right, culminating in the kidnapping and murder of the Christian Democrat ex-Prime Minister Aldo Moro in 1978 and the bomb in Bologna station in 1980. For most writers and intellectuals, these years marked a gradual end to the political activism that had characterized much, though not all, of the literature of the middle decades of the 20th century.

Yet the long post-war period of political stasis coincided with the most significant economic growth and concurrent social change in the country's history, reaching an apex during the years of the so-called 'Economic Miracle', 1958–62. Fuelled by the availability of labour in the south, economic growth caused massive internal migration from south to north, transforming the appearance and social complexion of the northern cities. With startling abruptness, what had been an economically backward, predominantly agricultural country joined the ranks of the world's advanced economies: by the late 1980s, Italy could claim to have wrested fifth place from the United Kingdom in terms of gross domestic product.

Then in the early 1990s, the post-war political system collapsed, as a result of corruption scandals, the fall of the Iron Curtain, and the emergence of new forces, in the first instance the Northern League, which claimed to speak up for the honest productive north that paid the bills of the corrupt and lazy south. In 1994, the media-mogul Silvio Berlusconi and his Forza Italia party brought about a complete redrawing of the Italian political map. Christian Democrat hegemony was replaced by Berlusconi's new coalition of the centre-right, including the extreme right Alleanza Nazionale, and the successors of the old Communist and Socialist parties joined up with some fringe parties to form a rather more unstable coalition of the centre-left. The eventual outcome has been something approaching a two-party system, though one under which the country has become even more divided politically than it was before. It seems a world away from *Il giardino dei Finzi-Contini* and World War II, even if many of the underlying issues and conflicts have remained.

* * *

In the chapters that follow, we look more closely at different ways in which writers have responded to the turbulent reality of Italian history, more recently and in the past. We shall see these in terms of two broadly opposed tendencies, sometimes both present in the same writer, and both deeply conditioned by historical circumstances. On the one hand, there is the tendency to withdraw into literature, as if it were a self-contained, self-regulating world cut off from ordinary experience, a tendency helped by the dispersal of writers across the regions and the absence of a metropolitan cultural centre. The 'lovers of art and poetry' whom Bassani mentions have often seen themselves and been seen as a caste apart, *letterati* in older parlance, intellectuals in modern times; Petrarch began the trend with his dismissals of the *vulgus*, the uneducated majority. This tendency is the subject of the next two chapters ('Tradition' and 'Theory'), the first of which traces the remarkably cohesive literary tradition that develops in contrast and in tension with the reality of regional dispersion and disunity. The following two chapters ('Politics' and 'Secularism') trace the opposite tendency, that of engagement with the reality of the times. To go back to Bassani again, the force of *Il giardino dei Finzi-Contini* depends very much on its combination of lyrical and evocative themes with a political narrative, but engagement with the world can also take the form of more broadly secular attitudes, in conflict particularly with the dominant Catholic religion. Our final chapter ('Women') brings together the two opposed tendencies we have been discussing, by considering the contrast between the very traditional representations of women by male writers, and women's negotiation of voices for themselves.

Our picture of Italian literature is, however, a picture of previous centuries, including the 20th, and is less applicable to the 21st. There has been a revolution in the political landscape, while in many ways the country as a whole has encountered the same economic and social problems as the rest of Europe, and achieved the same sort of modernity. As a result, even the writers of the late 20th century are no longer the presences they once were, and the younger writers who have come to the fore in the present century have quite different agendas. Many of the issues that we are concerned with in this book have simply lost the urgency that they had until relatively recently; Italian literature has become much more like that of other European countries, and much less concerned with the perhaps impossible task of keeping distinctively Italian traditions alive. We refer to the most recent

Italian writing from time to time, but we concentrate largely on literature written and published before 1990.

The literature we are concerned with is nothing like as monolithic as nationalist tradition wanted it to be, but it does have a distinctive character. It is a literature which dislikes intimacy and self-exposure and is suspicious of professions of sincerity, which likes to keep up form for form's sake when there is nothing else left, but which uses form and relative formality with ease and at times with great force, suppleness, and depth, which is constantly remaking the past to find ways through the crises of the present, and which in one way or another keeps ideas of humanity and human values firmly in view in the face of authoritarian dogma and power.

Chapter 2
Tradition

E la tradizione tramanda tramanda fa passamano

[And the tradition transmits transmits plays pass the parcel]
(Zanzotto)

In early 1917, Giuseppe Ungaretti, an unknown twenty-six-year-old poet who had published a first, very slight collection the previous year, was serving as a private in the Italian army facing the Austrians in the freezing cold of the mountains on Italy's northern borders. On 26 January, he wrote three short poems, the shortest of which, 'Mattina' ('Morning'), was to become one of the most famous, or notorious, poems of the century. It appears in all published editions as follows:

MATTINA
Santa Maria La Longa il 26 gennaio 1917

M'illumino
d'immenso

It is still striking more than ninety years later, and it is certainly not what an English reader would expect. There is none of Wilfred Owen's pity of war, though Ungaretti does do some of that in some poems. Instead, there is what looks at first sight like a jotting, or a postcard, complete with date and the name of the village near

4. Ungaretti at the front in 1916

Udine where the poem was written. Early readers wondered if it was a poem at all. The text itself – assuming it could be separated off from its heading – consists of just two substantial words plus two particles. Put together, the two lines formed a recognizable standard seven-syllable line, but Ungaretti has separated the two typographically, throwing the individual words into relief in what it was easy to feel was an arbitrary fashion. There is no rhyme in the normal Italian sense. If you do pick away at the sound texture,

23

or better still hear Ungaretti reciting the poem (there are recordings), you can register a phonic interplay and repetition between the two lines, with the 'e' of 'immenso' abruptly opening up the mouth in a way you could say corresponds to the sudden illumination the words refer to. But it is all on a disconcertingly minuscule scale, and disconcertingly put. You do not normally say in Italian 'I illuminate myself' any more than you do in English; 'd'immenso' looks like a phrase that should mean 'immensely', only such a phrase does not exist, and the reader is left wondering what to do with an adjective that has no noun to refer to ('with immense'), the instinctive solution being to naturalize the phrase by taking the sense to be 'the immense' or 'immensity'.

A sympathetic reader will probably argue that Ungaretti is actually releasing a range of imaginative possibilities through a brilliant act of poetic compression. This would have at its core one of those moments of illumination – here possibly as much willed as spontaneous – that have been a defining feature of European poetry since Romanticism: the example most familiar to English readers is Wordsworth's 'Daffodils'. Maybe we could argue that he is affirming the power of life and imagination in the face of death and destruction, though that is much less obviously the case with the other two poems he wrote that day.

That said, we might still feel we have missed something important. Or rather that the question of whether this is a poem at all is somehow central to what Ungaretti is doing. And however varied, the answers Ungaretti and Italian critics and readers have inevitably come up with all look at 'Mattina' in relation to other Italian poetry of his own time and the past, and see it, not just as a response to war, but as a response to what other poets had done and were doing. Among the figures who dominated the poetic landscape of the immediate past were Carducci and D'Annunzio, who Bassani mentioned at the start of *Il giardino dei Finzi-Contini* as having 'immortalized' Corso Ercole I d'Este in Ferrara. For the young Ungaretti, Carducci and D'Annunzio were both in their different ways extremely skilful with words and had done much to voice the aspirations of the new Italy, but they had lost sight of what poetry should really be about, striking grandiose bard-like postures inside and outside their writings, and too often substituting rhetoric for inspiration. Together with the more low-key Giovanni Pascoli, often joined with them in one of the literary triads that Italian criticism has always had a liking for, they seemed to represent an outmoded poetic tradition that modern Italy would do well to dispense with. This was the solution put forward with violent revolutionary enthusiasm by the Futurists, who as early as 1909 were demanding that the country embrace speed, machines, electricity, and every other aspect of modern life, and abandon everything traditional, not just in poetry and art, but eventually in almost everything else, from education (bombs in schools to harden the pupils up) to cooking (unprecedented mixtures of sweet and savoury ingredients).

Ungaretti flirted with Futurist ideas about getting rid of syntax and punctuation in poetry, but seems to have decided quite quickly that in practice Futurist poems were mostly sound and fury, with little depth or significance. The path he found himself following was to concentrate on whatever it was that made poetry poetry – some poetic essence or purity that was escaping both the Futurists and the late 19th-century poets – and to discard everything else. The results are evident in 'Mattina' and the other poems of what eventually would become his first major collection, *L'allegria* (*Gaiety*), published originally in 1919, but not given its definitive form and title until 1942. By then, Ungaretti was an established name and had theorized his practice, arguing that in *L'allegria* he had worked to recover the poetic power of the individual word, before moving on in his second book, *Sentimento del tempo* (*Feeling of Time*, 1933), to recover and renew poetic phrasing and metre.

Hermeticism, as this kind of poetry came to be known from its disdain for prose-meanings in the name of an arcane (hermetic) poetic purity that could at most be alluded to rather than stated, is Italy's form of European modernism. It owed a good few debts to Mallarmé, Valéry, and other French poets, but it was also intensely Italian. The poetic essences Ungaretti and his younger contemporaries looked for derived almost entirely from the Italian tradition, not as it had been practised in the later 19th century, but as it had been shaped by its greatest figures: Leopardi from the early 19th century and then much further back to the 14th, Petrarch looming especially large. It is not just that a certain tone in Ungaretti echoes Leopardi or Petrarch, but that the actual words he uses are ones that they either used or, one feels, might have used. The adventurousness and the modernity lie in what is done with the words in a poem such as 'Mattina', not in flamboyant choices of vocabulary.

* * *

Ungaretti looks back into the Italian tradition, and does so in a very traditional way. Historically, Italian poetry has gone forward by constantly reshaping what has been done before, sometimes reacting against previous practice and assumptions, though much less frequently than in other countries, and with a surprisingly consistent willingness to recognize past excellence and to look for models further back, if ones closer to hand are found wanting. Conversely, and largely for the linguistic reasons sketched out in the previous chapter, Italian poetry has been cautious about drawing directly on contemporary spoken usage. Traditionalism of this sort has at times inhibited personal vision, and led to numbing conventionalism, but it also tends to promote continuity, coherence, and shared literary values across the centuries. At its best, the tradition has consciously assimilated the new into existing literary systems which themselves evolve slowly over time. The fundamental pattern is laid down by the founding fathers of Italian poetry, Dante and Petrarch. Both are immensely original, but their originality is deeply bound up with their own assimilation of preceding literature. Both are immensely influential, though of the two, it is Petrarch who is a more consistent presence over the centuries, in part because of his own assimilation and mediation of Dante.

Dante's first book, the *Vita nova* (*New Life* or *Young Life*), is grounded in personal experience. It tells the story of his love for the woman he calls Beatrice, who historically was probably a Florentine girl called Bice Portinari and who died in 1290, not long before the book was completed. But Dante enriches the literary Beatrice immeasurably by deleting or muting the historical context and concentrating on her resonances against other *donne*, that is *dominae* or ladies, who figure in medieval poetry, and against allegorizations of female figures in the Bible and beyond. At the same time, inseparably from the account of his love, Dante offers a representation of his growth as poet, from conventional beginnings to becoming the creator and principal voice of what he would later call the *dolce stil novo*, the 'sweet new style', with which he and his friend Guido Cavalcanti took Tuscan lyric poetry to new musical and intellectual heights. Literary self-consciousness increases still more in subsequent works, with a theorization of allegorical poetry in the *Convivio* (*The Banquet*, 1304–7), and with an assessment of Italian, French, and Provençal lyric poetry in the *De vulgari eloquentia* (*On Vernacular Eloquence*, 1303–5). The *Divine Comedy* (?1307–21), originally probably entitled simply the *Commedia*, includes among its many strands Dante's poetic genealogy, with Virgil as prime but not sole poetic father, though it then moves on to assert and demonstrate its author's great originality. We shall discuss it mainly in Chapter 4.

The same dynamic is evident in Petrarch, writing a generation after Dante and feeling obliged to deal with his enormous threatening presence, as well as with a host of other writers he found it much easier to embrace. Petrarch does not construct for himself a genealogy on Dante's lines, preferring to assert his individuality as a writer; yet he was an outright classicizer, adapting his name to Petrarca in place of his patronymic

Petracchi, and borrowing from Horace and Seneca his favourite image of his way of working, a bee taking pollen from many flowers to fuse into its own specific honey. Most of his writings are in Latin, a large and varied body of work, covering history, biography, epic poetry, verse letters, pastoral poetry, allegorical dialogues, polemical tracts, and semi-philosophical treatises. Everything is saturated with his reading, and everything is personal, including his epic, the *Africa*, which is ostensibly concerned with the struggle of Rome to defeat Hannibal in the late 3rd century BC, but which is simultaneously an arena in which Petrarch debates his own and his contemporaries' literary and spiritual dilemmas. The same is true of his lyric poetry, the main form of literature he produced in Italian, a triumphal re-writing of Dante and his predecessors which establishes a standard and style for Italian poetry that subsequent poets can never wholly ignore. The principal work is the collection of 366 poems which Petrarch's original manuscript entitles the *Rerum vulgarium fragmenta Francisci Petrarce laureati poete* (literally, the 'fragments of vernacular matters of Francis Petrarch, laureate poet'), which has been more conveniently known since the 16th century as the *Canzoniere* (originally a generic term for song-book) or *Rime* (*Rhymes*). Otherwise, in Italian, there are only some uncollected poems, some drafts and fragments, and the not quite finished sequence of allegorical *Triumphi* (*Triumphs*), which were widely read until the 16th century but have since fallen out of favour, largely because of their insistent erudition.

Almost all the poems centre on Petrarch's love for a woman he called Laura, who, like Beatrice, may have had a historical existence, but is transformed into something and someone else in the poetry: a beautiful figure with golden hair who can appear as courtly lady, nymph, goddess, girl, projection of the imagination, emblem of poetry itself, or an empty name. To this figure Petrarch remains devoted (at least in his poems) from the moment he first saw her in the Church of St Clare in Avignon on Good Friday 1327, to her death on the same day in 1348 – the year of the Black Death which included some of Petrarch's closest friends among its victims – and then for ten years and more after that. It is an unusually prolonged affair even for medieval poetry, and is almost certainly in part cast as it is in response to Dante's projection of Beatrice in the *Vita nova* and later in the *Divine Comedy*. The *donna* as Beatrice had been a solution, leading Dante to salvation; as Laura, she becomes the problem. Petrarch is never sure that he has got her or his desires into an acceptable focus. Is she, or her beautiful image, distracting him from serious matters, first and foremost from thinking about the ultimate fate of his soul? Or at the other extreme, does she or her image offer moral stimulation and ultimately a foretaste of divine beauty and goodness? Or is the reality different from either? Petrarch's poems unendingly debate such issues, finding no answers beyond the need to turn away from the world and throw himself on God's mercy: the long poem concluding the *Canzoniere* is an appeal for help from the Virgin Mary, not a total renunciation.

It is deeply personal poetry, debating issues which are at the centre of the many Latin works in which Laura has no place at all, but everything is blended from Petrarch's reading. The more angelic and abstract forms of Laura are anticipated in the *dolce stil novo*, the sweet new style identified by Dante; more sensual moments draw on the Provençal troubadour Arnaut Daniel; Laura as nymph and goddess comes from Horace and Ovid; the ethical debates reflect a highly individual interpretation of St Augustine. Amazingly (though later readers may forget how amazing it is), there is no sense of pastiche. One of the most powerful poems (264) concludes: 'E veggio 'l meglio et al peggior m'appiglio' ('I see the better course and stick to the worse'). The line is a close reworking of a famous epigram from Ovid's *Metamorphoses* (VII, 20–1), but it is, we feel, entirely Petrarch both in sentiment and in the architecture of its antitheses. Here, as elsewhere, classicism blends with the practice of the medieval love lyric, with a new, more resonant music and a new stylistic assurance. In complete contrast to the existential hesitations that they voice, the poems move seamlessly between conversational ease, patent artifice, and high formality. The very forms that Petrarch uses had almost all existed in Italian poetry since its beginnings in Sicily. The sonnet may have been invented by the Sicilian Giacomo da Lentini in the mid-1220s, and had been used by every poet of note, and by every merchant or noble who tried his hand at Italian verse, over the following hundred years. The 317 sonnets in the *Canzoniere* normally use what by Petrarch's time had become the standard scheme: two quatrains, each rhyming ABBA, followed by two tercets using various patterns of two or three rhymes. Yet Petrarch's endlessly varied deployment of the form combines intricacy, balance, dynamic movement, and a final completeness in a way that no previous poet (not even Dante) had come close to, with such mastery that it is as the Petrarchan sonnet that the form comes to be known and imitated throughout Europe. As for the *canzone* – nowadays any kind of song but in the Middle Ages a lengthy and complex form of much greater prestige than the sonnet – Petrarch's 29 instances demonstrate a range and depth that none of his successors approach. It is perhaps unsurprising that most keep to the sonnet and other shorter forms that he had used.

Other poets were already drawing on Petrarch during his lifetime and continued to do so over the next hundred years or so, though in a quite free, not to say casual, way. This was partly because serious writers continued as Petrarch had done to think that the real medium for poetry and intellectual discourse was classical Latin, and that writing in the vernacular was at best a pastime, an attitude strongly reinforced by the pre-eminence of classical humanism in the 15th century. In the early 16th century, however, a consensus developed that Latin could not really be taken any further, and that significant writing could be created in vernacular Italian. The problem was what sort of writing and what sort of vernacular. The programme that eventually triumphed was that of Pietro Bembo, a Venetian cardinal, humanist scholar, and poet, who in his *Prose della volgar lingua* (*Writings on the Vernacular*

Language, 1525) put forward the thesis that if poetry and prose in Italian were to achieve excellence they must imitate the work of the most excellent writers, as was (Bembo claimed) the best practice in Latin. The Italian equivalents of Virgil and Cicero were in his view Petrarch and Boccaccio, the one offering a model for verse in the *Canzoniere*, the other a model for prose in the *Decameron*. This curious argument, so regressive and arbitrary in many ways, chimed with contemporary thinking in a way that alternatives did not. Its long-lasting influence over the subsequent course of Italian literature was then ensured by the Florentine Accademia della Crusca, founded in 1582, which used its influential dictionary, the *Vocabolario*, begun in 1591, to regulate the language of poetry and literary prose for the following two centuries and more. The result in poetry was detailed, often pedantic imitation of Petrarch's style and language, and, to some extent, a recycling of the figure of the Petrarchan lover, now often made thoroughly Neoplatonic (which Petrarch himself was not) by the aspiration to rise up from contemplation of the beloved to that of the supreme goodness and beauty of God. Thus a kind of base-line for what was acceptable as serious poetry was established, and the possibility of achieving it opened up through the availability, enhanced by the revolutionary new technology of print, of glossaries, rhyming dictionaries, and the manuals of which Bembo's own *Prose* was a forerunner. Literate Italians from any part of the peninsula, whatever local language they spoke, could learn to write good Italian sonnets, much as they learned how to write good Latin verse, and until at least the end of the 19th century, they would often manage both. Petrarchism has so often been criticized as deadeningly conventional, which it certainly could be, especially in its view of women; but it was also accessible and civilized.

* * *

The Petrarchan tradition of poetry did, of course, evolve. Its subject matter became much wider, with everything from political events to scientific discoveries joining the core thematics of serious and not

5. Giorgio Vasari, *Six Tuscan Poets*. Petrarch and Dante are in the foreground; Boccaccio is probably between and behind them. In reality, only Petrarch was actually crowned poet laureate

so serious love. The idiom itself successfully adapted to other forms of poetry, principally the epic. Ariosto revised his *Orlando furioso* (*The Madness of Orlando*, the third and final version of which was printed in 1532) to make the language fit with Bembo's doctrines, the final result showing no trace of the prolonged and painstaking efforts required. By the later 16th century, the linguistic issue was in effect resolved for all types of poetry, and poets and critics could and did concentrate more on issues of style and subject matter. The baroque phase that follows in the early 17th century has its supreme master in Giambattista Marino, who makes much of striking conceits and paradoxes in his lyrics and in his narrative poem

Adone (1623), where they all but submerge the story of Venus and Adonis which is the ostensible subject. The baroque then gives way to a return to classical and Petrarchan purism. At the forefront of this was the Accademia dell'Arcadia, founded in 1690, and inspired by Jacopo Sannazaro's immensely popular pastoral novel *Arcadia* (1504), which gave canonical formulation for the whole of Europe to a mythic world of nymphs and shepherds, remote from the complexities of life if not from all its woes. Arcadia's linguistic and stylistic standards and its particular bent for pastoral scenery and imagery became the norm for at least the following hundred years, but by the end of the 18th century, the pressures for some form of renewal had become intense. The Romantic *manifesti*, which were published by Ludovico di Breme and other Milanese writers soon after Napoleon's fall in 1815, make what look on the surface like sensible demands. Literature (that is, primarily poetry) should reject classical mythology and open itself up to the 'people' through writing in popular language on issues of real concern to readers. But the movement was limited to Milan, its aspirations unrealizable in a dialect-speaking country, and its protagonists, none of them outstandingly talented, were silenced, often brutally, by the Austrian regime. Renewal, when it did come, was achieved by standing back from Romantic ideas rather than by embracing them.

Italy's greatest 19th-century poet recreates and updates the figure of the Petrarchan scholar and poet. Isolated and miserable in the small town of Recanati in the Marche, Count Giacomo Leopardi devoured and extended the large family library, becoming one of the foremost scholars of classical literature and contemporary thought in Europe, and developing a radical materialist pessimism of his own which dominates both his prose writings and his poetry. Leopardi ridicules the main literary theses of the Italian Romantics and argues for imitation of the ancients, who he claims were admirable because they had managed in their art to imitate nature in a way that eluded the moderns. Rather than fill in complex details when describing a subject, they preferred simplicity, suggestion, and musicality. The results of such an approach can be seen in his slim volume of *Canti* (*Songs*). These thirty-six poems, written mostly in groups between 1817 and Leopardi's death in 1837, constitute a powerful re-casting of the Italian tradition, embracing both the highly formal *canzone* and the freer, more personal poems with country settings which he called *idilli*, after the ancient Greek genre of the idyll, and merging the two together in novel ways in his later work. The opening of 'La sera del dí di festa' ('The evening before the holiday'), one of the early idylls, is famous:

> Dolce e chiara è la notte e senza vento
> e queta sovra i tetti e in mezzo agli orti
> posa la luna.
> [The night is sweet and clear and windless
> and quietly above the rooftops and among the orchards
> the moon rests.]

The words are almost trite, the phrasing apparently casual, almost prosaic, the basic image a Romantic commonplace, the tones almost familiarly Petrarchan. Yet these lines have been felt (rightly) to be among the most affecting in Italian poetry, precisely because they have the musicality, simplicity, and power of suggestion that Leopardi admired. It was to lines like these that poets and critics of the early 20th century looked when they talked of absolute poetic essences. We shall come back in Chapter 3 to Leopardi's thought.

But Petrarch was not enough of a model or inspiration for the tumultuously revolutionary 19th century, let alone for the century that followed. To Romantic and post-Romantic readers, his poetry could easily seem artificial and restrictive, his career one of weak-kneed adaptation to circumstances and the demands of patrons. In his stead came Dante, heroic, suffering exile, with moral, political, and literary lessons in abundance for the contemporary citizen and poet. This was something new. In English-speaking countries, Dante is viewed as a towering figure of world literature, and we might expect to see his influence everywhere in the literature of Italy. In fact, however much admired, the *Divine Comedy* was difficult for writers to assimilate. Petrarch holds the poem at a distance in what many modern readers have felt to be an ungenerous way, and absorbs what he does absorb from it into the fabric of his own poetry, without any more acknowledgement than he gives to other previous authors he might echo. The poetic tradition follows in his wake in this regard as in much else. Various didactic poems were written under the influence of the *Divine Comedy* in the decades immediately following Dante's death in 1321, but then they fade away. Dante's poem does not fit into or create a literary genre, nor did it conform to accepted ideals of classical decorum. However lofty his thought, Dante's way of writing did not accord with Bembo's vision of the high style. At one or two moments, it was palpably vulgar; at others, it was too erudite and Latinate; more generally, it was too rough, too unmusical, too individual – in fact, overall, it was all those things that readers of the Romantic period were ready to rediscover, and which modern readers tend to think are essential to great poetry.

Not that Dante had been forgotten in the centuries immediately after his death. His status is evident from the abundance of commentaries on the *Comedy* which began to appear (in Italian and Latin) less than ten years afterwards and continued into the Renaissance. In the 14th and 15th centuries, Dante also fed into a way of writing verse that was opposed to Petrarchism and to high poetry in general. This is now usually called *poesia giocosa* ('playful poetry'), and while not all of it is deliberately humorous, its idiom is often called 'comic', following Dante's idiosyncratic use of the term to refer to a mixture of styles of the kind he practised in the *Divine Comedy*. The earliest *poesia giocosa* appears in Florence in the later 13th century and then quickly spreads to other cities of central Italy. The most famous early practitioner is Cecco Angiolieri of Siena, who gives a personal twist to themes well established in medieval goliardic poetry – gambling, shortage of money, and lust for a harridan anti-Beatrice called Bettina. Italian criticism stresses the literariness of all this, but there may be at least an element of lived experience. Subsequent comic poetry – often in Dante's *terza rima* when it was not in one form or another of the sonnet – became almost as rigid in its rules as high poetry, though it could be used for coded satire (for instance, of the Church), or for other forms of in-group allusiveness to which the Petrarchan style did not easily lend itself.

We may wonder that more poets did not break through the constraints of tradition and, especially if we are English speakers, we may be pleasantly surprised when we come to a poet like Michelangelo who seems to do just that. Michelangelo achieves in his verse some of the force and individuality of his painting and sculpture. Many of the poems are as contorted stylistically as Michelangelo claimed, in one poem, that his body had become while painting the Sistine Chapel ceiling. They may reflect in their form his Neoplatonic struggles to rise up to the divine from the earthly beauty he sees in the young aristocrat Tommaso Cavalieri and, unless they are literary fictions, in occasional young women. Michelangelo is one of the Italian poets most translated into English over the last hundred and fifty years; Italian reception has always been more muted, beginning with the first edition of his poems produced by his nephew several decades after his death, which censored some poems, and in others regularized the metre, polished up the syntax and imagery, and generally assimilated Michelangelo to the prevalent classicism. Modern editions go back to the original manuscripts, but Italian critics tend still to see him as an interesting oddity, who poetically speaking re-works Petrarch rather than Dante, and who is equalled or outclassed as a lyric poet by Giovanni Della Casa and Torquato Tasso, both of whom work with rather than against the prevalent Petrarchism.

* * *

When Ungaretti wrote 'Mattina' and the other poems of *L'allegria*, therefore, he was performing a highly traditional poetic manoeuvre, and his aim was not to destroy but to help renew and re-affirm the central tradition of Italian poetry. Yet there is something forced about the process. It is significant that hermeticism flourished under Fascism, and had the full support of the regime, in spite of demands from Fascist hard-liners for a poetry which did more to articulate the values of Mussolini's revolution. By the time the regime collapsed, most hermetic poets had moved on to discover other kinds of poetry, generally of a less exclusive kind, and in the immediate post-war decades many attempted more overt political commitment (*impegno*), almost always to values and policies of the Left. Yet the issue of tradition has recurred again and again in the often fiercely polemical debates about poetry that run from Futurism to the neo-avant-garde (*Neoavanguardia*) of the 1960s. Andrea Zanzotto's line quoted at the head of this chapter, from a poem in his 1968 collection *La beltà* (*Beauty*), leaves ironically unclear what is in the parcel that tradition keeps passing on. Modernism, sometimes flamboyantly unconventional as it is in much of Zanzotto, certainly continued to be one of its main strands, and has proved strong enough to assimilate ostensible revolutionaries such as the neo-avant-garde's most prominent poet, Edoardo Sanguineti. At the same time, poets have drawn increasingly on French, German, American, and other literatures, not to mention showing (as Zanzotto does, for instance) that it is possible to write serious poems in dialect.

The 20th-century poet who has come increasingly to be seen as embodying the most thoughtful and poetically satisfying response to the issue of tradition is Eugenio Montale, who may have wrenched it in unexpected directions in his earlier poetry, but did keep it alive into the second half of the 20th century. There was a time when he was bracketed with Ungaretti as a hermetic poet. In fact, from his first collection, *Ossi di seppia*, of 1925, he eschewed extreme modernism and incorporated into his verse a strongly discursive, rational element. Contemporary critics tended to see this as 'prosa', that jostled with the moments of 'poesia' embodied in the 'cuttlefish bones' of the title. The contrast

6. Italian poets react to Edoardo Sanguineti's avant-garde poems. From the top left to right: Ugo Foscolo, Alessandro Manzoni, Giosuè Carducci, Giacomo Leopardi, Gabriele D'Annunzio, Giovanni Pascoli, Giuseppe Ungaretti, and Eugenio Montale

has lost its force, however, and Montale is now viewed as bringing into Italian poetry a welcome harshness of style and broadness of vision, which seem to correspond more fully with modern experience than Ungaretti's minimalism. Not that he is any less literary, though his ultimate stylistic point of reference is Dante rather than Petrarch, and then, when he shifts into love poetry in the 1930s and 1940s, the Italian medieval tradition as a whole. For the beloved, and the poetry associated with her, become for a time the one source of positive values and inner strength to set against the sheer destructiveness of World War II. It was in the context of the time a difficult perspective. It was implicitly anti-Fascist and by degrees became explicitly so – Montale was the first of Italy's recognized poets to risk publishing, if on a very minor scale, poetry that went against Fascist dogma. But its privileging of the personal and the private over the collective and the public also ran counter to notions of *impegno*, disorienting left-wing activist writers such as Franco Fortini and Pierpaolo Pasolini who found themselves admiring Montale's work as poetry but disapproving of it politically. A silence followed his third collection, *La bufera e altro* (*The Storm and Other Things*, 1956), which many thought marked the conclusion of his career as a poet. Then in 1971 came a new and surprising beginning with *Satura*. The title means 'medley' and the collection is by turns conversational, satirical, argumentative, paradoxical, self-mocking, and humorous. Here and in the unexpectedly large body of work that followed, Montale writes about the modern world from the point of view of a bleakly sceptical, liberal-minded conservative, with doubts even about his own work, which he seems to suggest may not be poetry at all, but an anti-poetry which is all that it is now possible to write.

* * *

Poetry is now mostly read educationally or pursued as a minority interest in Italy, as elsewhere in Europe, but historically it enjoyed a privileged position in the hierarchy of literary genres. The novel in particular had more of a struggle to establish itself in Italy than in France and England, in part because of a mind-set which was suspicious of a modern hybrid genre with no particular rules to it.

One of the ways of validating a novelist until very recently was to speak of him (more rarely, her) as a 'poeta', as if the imaginative value of any literary work lay principally in its lyric qualities. It was still felt necessary as late as the 1930s to defend the novel *vis-à-vis* the claims of lyric poetry, tragedy, and epic. Though the latter two were by then practised only by writers with delusions of Fascist grandeur, the 19th century had seen a profusion of verse tragedies, now mostly unreadable, which had played a part in Risorgimento unrest. Before beginning work on the *Promessi sposi*, Manzoni had been a lyric poet and then moved on to tragedy. His great novel took him more than twenty years to complete; even when it was finished and had become a European success, he remained uncertain about whether the sort of combination of history and fiction he had achieved was justifiable. Many of his successors would feel obliged to think through in similar ways what they doing in fiction.

The problems of the novelist in Italy throughout the 19th century, and for the greater part of the 20th, were also to do with the traditional view of the language of prose, compounded by the real limits of literacy in the population. With most Italians being dialect-speaking peasants who did not or could not read, and a numerically exiguous, also dialect-speaking, middle class, the market for the novel in Italy was obviously much smaller than in northern Europe. At one moment in the *Promessi sposi*, Manzoni speaks of having twenty-five readers; he was being knowingly modest, of course, but in many ways he had to create a readership, rather than finding one ready-made. He had in a sense to create a language too, and it was largely this which made him take so long to write the novel. To grasp the problem, we must again look back to Bembo's injunction that the contemporary author who wanted to write good prose should imitate Boccaccio, just as the contemporary poet should imitate Petrarch. Bembo had set out a full grammar derived from Boccaccio and proposed that so far as possible vocabulary too should be grounded in Boccaccio's usage. The general adoption of Bembo's ideas meant that already in the later 16th century Italian prose was often remote from any of the varieties of spoken language to be found in the peninsula, except perhaps in some of the princely courts; Florentine too had moved on from the forms of language which Boccaccio used in the mid-14th century. Besides, even in the raciest stories of the *Decameron*, the style is elaborated in accordance with the rules of medieval rhetoric, with forays into popular speech only in comic dialogue. Bembo and the writers who followed him gave the rhetoric a more classical aura but unhesitatingly concurred with Boccaccio's assumptions. For two centuries after Bembo, literary prose was almost as static as verse. Innovation was strictly regulated by the Accademia della Crusca, though there were transient fads for first Spanish and then French importations. When Manzoni embarked on the composition of a realist historical novel in 1819, he thus faced enormous difficulties. It was not just that the peasants and artisans he wanted to represent did not use the vocabulary, grammar, and syntax of literary Italian, but that the language in which he could conduct the narrative was more suited to oratory and essay-writing. It was rich in abstractions, but poor in concrete vocabulary, and had an overwhelmingly outdated air.

His solution was bizarre in some ways and also brilliant, especially for a French-educated Milanese: it was to immerse himself in the usage of contemporary Florence. Manzoni could argue that the speech of its inhabitants continued the linguistic heritage of Dante, Petrarch, and Boccaccio. He modernized standard Italian prose accordingly, preserving the intellectual suppleness of the best Italian writing of the 18th-century Enlightenment, but taking from contemporary Florentine the sort of concreteness, range, and idiomatic vitality that literary Italian appeared to have lost. At the same time, he performed a neat sleight of hand to justify representing non-Florentines as speaking his renovated national language. His novel is set in 17th-century Lombardy and pretends to be based on an anonymous chronicle of the time that Manzoni has translated and adapted for modern readers. In this translated form, it is almost plausible for his Lombards of almost two centuries earlier to speak 19th-century Florentine.

Manzoni produced a great novel, on which we shall have more to say in Chapter 4, but his form of modernization provided a stimulus rather than a model. Other than for historical prestige, there was no particular reason to privilege contemporary Florentine. In many ways, Manzoni's practice was easily assimilated into traditional literary assumptions and practice, which proved as tenacious as other traditions in a predominantly conservative country. Thus until well after World War II, almost every novelist of any stature felt obliged to contend with the language issue, and was often evaluated, negatively or positively, on linguistic and stylistic grounds. But modernization did gradually gather force. Verga, whom we also look at further in Chapter 4, discarded the Florentine project in order to create a new language which seems to present the reader with the colour and rhythms of Sicilian speech, without resorting to dialect forms, though the coincidences with actual usage are in fact limited. That was one way forward. Other novelists played with the possibilities that dialect offered.

In the mid-20th century, Carlo Emilio Gadda deliberately mixed literary and scientific Italian with Milanese and Roman dialect to reflect what he saw as the baroque confusion of the world; Pasolini used a discordant mixture of Italian and Roman dialect in his novels about the Roman underclass. But by then, a modern narrative prose language was firmly established, with writers like Svevo and Pirandello, both of whom leave *poesia* and stylistic experimentation aside. Svevo's *La coscienza di Zeno*, for instance, both lacks any obvious linguistic colour, and deploys quite complex sentence-forms that many early readers thought cumbersome and uninspired, though it is actually of a piece with the complexity of his vision as an artist. Yet his language is far from colloquial: convincing representations of actual speech, whether popular or not, appear only with the Neorealists after World War II, and even then the impulse remains strong to make them literary in one way or another.

With prose as with poetry, the sense of a single central tradition has fallen away in recent decades, as the whole language issue has lost its urgency. A highly wrought manner is just one of the options open to the contemporary writer, for writers in Italy as in other countries. So too is a simple style, though yet again this may have a literary hinterland. Gianni Celati, for instance, uses simple structures and the sparest lexicon in his later stories, but he has in mind the kind of *novella* that was written in Italy before Boccaccio. Conversely, the most successful novelist of the 1990s, Andrea Camilleri, regularly uses pastiches of Sicilian and Italian that readers from the whole length of Italy find they can understand and enjoy, but behind him are the examples of Gadda and Pasolini. The past is not completely deleted. It is only that it tends to return in muted, approachable forms.

The awareness of tradition is therefore one aspect of the tendency of literature to withdraw into itself which we referred to at the end of the last chapter. In the next chapter, we shall trace another, closely related aspect of this tendency: the intense concern with the ideas that underlie literature and its traditions. Italian writers have always had a fascination with theory, with abstract models of literary form or content. We shall examine how theory and practice interact in some of Italy's major writers: theory in the sense both of ideas about the nature of literature and how it should be written, and of ideas about man and the world. Sometimes over-cerebral or academic, the theoretical bent can exacerbate the separation of literature from ordinary life; but at its best it produces a highly productive interplay between abstract formulation, imaginative creativity, and responses to the real world.

Chapter 3
Theory

E di nemica ella divenne amante

[She who was once a foe became his lover]
(Tasso)

Torquato Tasso's epic poem *Gerusalemme liberata* (*Jerusalem
Delivered* or *The Liberation of Jerusalem*) was published in 1581
without his consent and still in his view unfinished, during the
long period in which, on account of his paranoid behaviour, he
was locked up in an asylum by his patron, the last Duke of Ferrara.
It was preceded by the *Discorsi dell'arte poetica* (*Discourses on the
Poetic Art*), an acute and refined theoretical discussion of epic
subject matter, structure, and style. These first *Discorsi* were then
obsessively revised and extended as the *Discorsi del poema eroico*
(*Discourses on the Heroic Poem*), which appeared in 1594
immediately after the *Gerusalemme conquistata* (*Jerusalem
Conquered*), the finished and extended version of his epic. But
while the theory in the two books of *Discorsi* remains substantially
the same, the second poem comes much closer to it than the first:
there are major elements of the *Liberata* which the theory does
not account for, and which in the *Conquistata* are substantially
reduced. It is largely as a result of this mismatch between theory
and practice that the first poem, not the second, is read today and
has been read since Tasso's time: the features that the theory does

not account for are a major source of the attraction that has drawn readers to the poetry.

This difference between the theory and practice, and to a lesser extent between the two poems, mainly concerns the matter of love. The principal subject of both poems, the siege and capture of Jerusalem in the First Crusade, matches the essentially classical view of the epic that the two books of *Discorsi* propose. So too does the language: Tasso's principles of magnificence, roughness (*asprezza*), and energy recreate for Italian the Roman idea of the high poetic style, and are faithfully followed in the poems. But there is little in the *Discorsi* that corresponds to the central and very unclassical position that love occupies in the *Liberata* and, if much less so, in the *Conquistata* as well. The amorous, indeed erotic, relations between the two Christian champions, Rinaldo and Tancredi, and their pagan female opponents, Armida and Clorinda, are not incidental episodes (which the theory allows for), but pivotal elements in the plot, as crucial obstacles to the fulfilment of the Crusaders' mission; the poems are not just about the conflict between Christians and Saracens, but also about the conflict between duty and love.

At the same time, in the *Liberata* in particular, the view of love is itself deeply complex and ambiguous. Tasso condemns love as a dereliction of duty, yet he has a remarkable, almost Romantic, ability to involve himself in his characters' feelings. Tancredi's tragic passion for Clorinda is described with great lyrical force, as is the hopeless love of a third Saracen, Erminia, for Tancredi. Love is mostly unrequited, and full of conflict, uncertainty, and anguish, reaching its extreme point when Tancredi fails to recognize Clorinda on the battlefield and kills her. In the one, exceptional, case of love between two Christians, Olindo and Sofronia, Olindo's declaration takes place at the stake, where he is bound back to back with his beloved and she has all her thoughts on heaven. The almost turbid sexuality implicit in these episodes is given particular force and suggestiveness in the figure of the proud and beautiful enchantress Armida. To help the Saracen cause, she seduces Rinaldo from his duty and carries him off to a sexual idyll on her magic island, and there the roles are reversed: in the line at the head of this chapter, 'she who was once a foe became his lover', and when he abandons her to take up his duty once more, it is love that makes her run after him. This last turn of events, the most dramatic illustration of the extent to which Tasso departed from his own rules in the *Liberata*, is almost entirely excised from the *Conquistata*.

Almost all literary production rests on some combination of practice and theory, and some degree of mismatch between them is the general rule. But in Tasso's case, the mismatch is particularly striking, and its consequences exceptional. It also reflects the intellectual climate of the middle and later 16th century. The

7. Nicolas Poussin, *Rinaldo and Armida*. One of the moments in Tasso's *Gerusalemme liberata* which has always appealed to readers is when his pagan enchantress falls passionately in love with her intended victim

consensus that developed from the end of the century before, that the vernacular could serve as the medium for serious literature, meant giving it, or trying to give it, the status of literature in Latin. In the course of the 16th century, there was a huge proliferation of theories of how this was to be achieved. Tasso's theories were distinguished both by their intellectual quality, and by the fact that, unusually, they helped to produce great literature. Very often, these theories were produced and debated in the new academies, not teaching institutions but gatherings of writers and thinkers which served as repositories of a learned classicizing culture that typically privileged rule creation and imitation. The earliest were fairly informal, such as the so-called Platonic Academy, a rather loose group that came into being in Florence in the 1460s around Marsilio Ficino and with the support of Lorenzo de' Medici; later ones were more institutional. The most influential of all, the Accademia della Crusca, subjected Tasso's language in the *Liberata* to vigorous criticism, even though, in a way illustrative both of the age and of his own tortured personality, he had submitted drafts for vetting by an informal committee of distinguished *letterati*.

* * *

Theorizing about literature by Italian writers goes back at least to Dante's *Vita nova*, as we pointed out in the previous chapter, and was articulated in depth in his subsequent prose works. Here the reflection is retrospective, but at the same time seems to act as a springboard for further movements forward. The most startling of these is the *Divine Comedy*, which marks a radical break with Dante's past work, in language and subject matter, and where the gap between theory and practice yawns wide, even wider than in Tasso's case. The purpose of the *Comedy* is explained, and its allegory analysed, in a letter addressed to his patron Can Grande della Scala, which may or may not be by Dante himself, but which probably reflects in some degree his conception of the poem. What the letter does not do is to furnish an adequate entry into the *Comedy*, even for 14th-century commentators. Almost all modern readers find that the poem itself is a much better guide to its meaning or meanings.

With Petrarch and Boccaccio the relationship of theory and practice becomes even more ambiguous, especially in relation to writing in the vernacular. Petrarch justified classical poetry as having some of the qualities of history and philosophy; through the device of allegorical interpretation, Boccaccio could even propose the idea of an essential harmony between classical poetry and theology. However, neither applies this kind of theorizing to his own writing. Petrarch's views on metre, style, and subject matter in Italian poetry have to be teased out of his practice, as does any theory of story-telling in Boccaccio. Petrarch often writes of his own work, in Latin as well as Italian, as if it rests on no other basis than the need for self-expression – even if he was probably not saying what he really thought when he dismissed his Italian poems as youthful trifles, nor was Boccaccio when he declared in the *Decameron* that he was writing just to chase away the melancholy of women. Subsequent writing in the vernacular in the 15th century is closer to Petrarch and Boccaccio in this regard than to Dante. But when explicit theorization became the norm in the following century, it proved remarkably durable, in part because of the academies. Romantics would see these as by-words for reaction and escapism, and point particularly to the Accademia dell'Arcadia and the cult of Arcadia that it fostered from the end of the 17th century. Branches of the Academy spread throughout the country, with members adopting fanciful shepherds' names and vying with each other in the composition of elegant pastoral verse. Yet Arcadia kept Renaissance ideas about literature alive and proved to be one of the main avenues by which new scientific and philosophical ideas entered Italian culture.

Much 18th-century theorizing about literature re-works established formulae, but not all. Carlo Goldoni, the major Italian dramatist before Pirandello, was a member of Arcadia, assuming the name of Polisseno Fegejo, by no means outlandish by Arcadian standards. As a practising playwright, over a period of time he took slapstick, obscenity, and improvisation out of the popular *commedia dell'arte*, individualized its stock characters (the so-called masks, though not all wore actual masks), and produced a new literate comedy of manners that his bourgeois Venetian public were happy to take their daughters to; they felt it reflected their mistrust of the idle, backward-looking aristocracy, and their own ethos of hard work and social stability. Goldoni explained his view of theatre after he had become established, principally in the preface he wrote for the published edition of sixteen of his plays, and then in the not quite performable programme-play, *Il teatro comico* (*Comic Theatre*, 1750). He re-wrote earlier successes, such as *Il servitore di due padroni* (*The Servant of Two Masters*), to make them fit better, but by and large, theory and practice coincide without effort, perhaps in part because Goldoni is happy to stay within the limits he set himself in his most famous plays such as *La locandiera* (*The Landlady*), or in dialect (which he treated more colourfully than Italian) *Sior Todero brontolon* (*Signor Todero the Grumbler*). Only in later plays (such as the *Villeggiatura* trilogy on the fashion for villa holidays) does the tone darken into a critique of middle-class hypocrisy and pretension, by which time Venice was teetering towards its final crisis as an independent state and the happy reciprocity between playwright and audience, theory and practice, came to an end.

Classicism did not die with the Romantics. As late as the mid-19th century, Carducci makes a polemical case for its thorough restoration, but by then the theorization of literature had generally moved away from classical prescription, following the changes in approach and sensibility of the Romantic era. As in the rest of Europe, theory becomes a part of the process of literary renovation, although some of the major theoretical movements, ranging from Romanticism itself to Futurism in the early 20th century, and then to the neo-avant-garde of the 1960s, produced manifestos that outshone their literary creations. At the same time, from the 19th century onwards, theory of a different kind comes to the forefront: as well as reflecting about literature, writers reflect at least as energetically on abstract general ideas of the world and human beings, and incorporate these thoughts into their work. This is notably true of two of the great figures of the 19th and early 20th centuries, Leopardi and Pirandello. Both develop sophisticated theories of literature; both also give voice to a complex range of feelings. But both set feeling in the context of a vision of life and literature which they articulate intellectually, often playing off the robust harshness of their thought against emotional delicacy or sentimentality, and deriving some of their most powerful effects from the clashes that result.

* * *

Leopardi was a professed anti-Romantic with the knowledge and acumen to articulate a challenging version of theoretical classicism, though paradoxically his view of the imagination and the individual is fairly typical of Romanticism in the general European sense. From the age of twenty-one, he kept a kind of intellectual diary, which he later called his *Zibaldone* (*Commonplace Book*); in it, he charted and developed his ideas as well as making scholarly notes on the ancient and modern authors he studied. The basis of his thinking, which was established early on and remained fundamentally unchanged throughout his life, was a radically materialist opposition between reason and imagination. Imagination produces all the goodness and beauty in life, which are only beneficial illusions that reason necessarily destroys; reason shows the world to be mere indifferent matter, unrelated and often opposed to the needs of human beings. We are fundamentally at the mercy of nature, that is, whatever creates and destroys things and living beings, with no purpose that we can understand and no concern for human happiness. Classical times were happier and more poetic because the ancients could believe in the beneficial illusions, whereas the so-called progress of reason has made it impossible for the moderns to do so. In the modern world, it is only in childhood and youth that these illusions can still subsist.

All of Leopardi's *Canti* are informed by this philosophical
pessimism, though his views on how to respond to what his
reason tells him undergo various changes of emphasis. The
youthful poems veer between grand philosophizing in the *canzoni*,
often through the personae of tragic classical figures, and
delicate evocations of the countryside with direct expressions of
emotional distress in the freer *idilli*. Then came a period of poetic
silence in which Leopardi concentrated his energies on the
philosophical *Operette morali* (*Short Moral Writings*), a collection
of prose-pieces, mostly in the form of dialogues between
historical, mythical, or imaginary figures, together with essays and
prose-poems that break up the despairing satirical tone of the
collection as a whole. When he comes back to poetry, all the
poems combine philosophical statement with description and
expressions of feeling. A second series of *idilli* juxtaposes
descriptive passages that contain some of Leopardi's most lyrical
and musical lines with bleakly curt expositions of their lessons for
the rational mind. One of these is Leopardi's most famous and
emblematic poem, 'A Silvia', in which the figure of the beautiful
and happy girl stands for everything that is beautiful and valuable
about the world, and her early death shows that all this is only a
youthful illusion that adult awareness cannot sustain. The *Canti*
celebrate love, virtue, youthful hope, and the beauty of nature, but
always with a sense of the essential transience and fragility that
modern, adult reason cannot help but perceive in them.

Leopardi's poetry thus attempts to wrest moral and aesthetic
values from a bleak pre-Darwinian vision. While much of it has to
settle for regret for what has been lost or can never be, in his later
poems he confronts the hostile forces of nature and time with
greater strength and candour. This 'titanism', as Italian critics call
it, reaches its summation in 'La ginestra'. The longest and most
powerful poem in the *Canti*, it concentrates the human situation
in the broom of the title, an innocent, beautiful, and modest
plant growing on the slopes of Vesuvius, at the mercy of the
unpredictable and mighty volcano. Lyrical passages alternate with

cutting denunciations of contemporary delusions, philosophical reflection, and appeals for human solidarity in the face of nature's brute power. Rational thought and action are here rehabilitated as the only defences we have, and illusion has become dangerous self-delusion. Not surprisingly, 'La ginestra' became a banner poem for many left-wing intellectuals in the mid-20th century.

Pirandello shared Leopardi's concern with the interaction of reason and illusion. His most extensive statement of his literary poetics, as well as his general philosophical vision, is *L'umorismo*, written originally in 1908, as a response to criticism of his novel *Il fu Mattia Pascal* by Benedetto Croce, who claimed that it mixed imagination or intuition and intellectual thought in a way that did justice to neither. At the heart of Pirandello's response is an opposition between 'life' and 'form' (*vita* and *forma*). Life, that is, reality, is an endless, essentially unknowable flux: anything that we think we know is simply a form that we project onto this. Truth is relative: people's view of the world outside them and of themselves is endlessly different, both between individuals and within a single individual; since all knowledge is illusion, no view is better than any other. This general philosophical position is the basis for Pirandello's literary theory, or rather the theory of a particular kind of literature which he calls *umorismo*. *Umorismo* is a kind of writing that can appear at any period and in any genre. It is related to what we would normally call humour, or sense of humour, but is more profound: it is the recognition that everything that we see or know or feel can also be seen or known or felt in the opposite way. It is this *sentimento del contrario*, the 'feeling for the opposite', intellectual and concrete at the same time, and both comic and tragic in its implications, that he argues underlies his work; it is not foisted onto the work, but is part and parcel of the original inspiration, a meaning that arises out of the image that founded the work, and one that is inseparable from that image.

That indeed is what happens in the best of the more than thirty plays that Pirandello wrote from 1915 to the end of his life. The drama arises from the characters' responses to the abnormal but very concrete situations in which they find themselves, either as a result of outside factors or through their own volition. The responses are direct, passionate, and frequently anguished, with only occasional forays into overt philosophizing. *Umorismo*, as Pirandello defines it, takes the form of the contrast between the way the characters see themselves, and the way other people see them; without necessarily putting the issue in philosophical terms, they thus find themselves confronting directly the fundamental problems of who they are and what they are doing in the world. One of Pirandello's best-known plays, *Enrico IV* (1922), is about a man who has definitely 'understood the game', as Pirandello puts it. The protagonist (his real name remains unknown) is a modern-day Italian who, having suffered for many years as a result of an accident from a mental illness that made him believe he was the medieval Emperor Henry IV, comes to his senses one day but decides to continue playing the same part. The 'humoristic' contrast of the work is that between the other characters' view that Henry is mad, and his own view that he is acting as he does for essentially rational reasons. He is only doing in a more consistent way what every individual does in life: playing a part. The difference is that he is doing it consciously, in a way that is both profound and heroic; the others, Pirandello implies, remain foolishly trapped by their illusory self-images.

Most of Pirandello's plays work with rather than against realist conventions, though the situations and the characters' motivations may be exceptional. But his most famous work, *Sei personaggi in cerca d'autore* (*Six Characters in Search of an Author*, 1921), subverts the conventions radically through the way it breaks down the customary distinction between off-stage reality and on-stage illusion. The six characters are represented as figures in a play which the author aborted as unsatisfactory, but who have somehow survived and now demand to have their drama brought to life on the stage. The play we are watching shows these fantastical figures (masked in some early productions) appearing at a rehearsal of another Pirandello play, and convincing the head of the troupe and his actors to try to put their drama on. The drama is scandalously melodramatic, involving coincidence, marital break-up, incest, suicide, and death of an innocent, and one can quite see why the 'author' rejected it. At the same time, the characters make a good case for being real in a way that the actors, the ostensibly real people, are not, having life perhaps but no constant form. This topsy-turvy vision of reality gives rise to often confusing interchanges, in which the characters live out scenes from their drama and the actors attempt clumsily to reproduce it.

The fantastical invention of this play (and then of two further, not quite so successful theatre-within-the-theatre plays) highlights Pirandello's favourite themes. The multiplicity of human personality and the impossibility of communication between people are demonstrated almost programmatically in a scene between two of the characters, the father and the stepdaughter, whose sexual services he tries to buy without knowing who she is. The interaction of characters and actors is also used to make a forceful critique of the theatre of the time, and at the same time, a critique of the theatre's inherent inability to be faithful to the author's original creation. But the most striking effect lies in the mutual interference between the outer play and the drama that is sporadically performed within it, the repeated back-and-forth movement between actors and characters, a dizzying, revolutionary manipulation of the audience's capacity to suspend disbelief, that makes the experience of the play, even today, a constant unanswered questioning as to what is real and what is not, and thus an experience in concrete and dramatic form of the theoretical principle of the relativity of truth.

* * *

The generation of writers that followed Pirandello seemed at first to move back to the characteristic realism of the late 19th century. The brilliant renewal of Italian fiction that occurred between the late 1930s and the mid-1960s was generally associated with Neorealism (*neorealismo*), the rather loose term applied originally to the films of Rossellini, De Sica, Visconti, and others that dealt directly and concretely with everyday life, usually from a left-wing standpoint, and often using non-professional actors. But while the leading novelists of this generation were intensely engaged with the reality of their time, they vigorously rejected the Neorealist label. Vittorini, Moravia, Calvino, and Pavese all aimed in their different ways both to include and to go beyond realism in the direction of more general levels of meaning, to unite intellectual ideas and imaginative vision – a tendency strongly encouraged by the predilection for abstract thought in Italian high culture of the period, the related assimilation of the role of the artist to that of the intellectual, and the conception, in Italy as elsewhere in Continental Europe, of intellectuals as a distinct social category. Moravia went so far as to envisage a form of 'essay-novel', a reflective, analytical tool for the investigation of modern life. We shall return to Vittorini, Moravia, and Calvino in later chapters, and focus here on Cesare Pavese, the troubled novelist and poet who committed suicide in a hotel room in his native Turin in 1950, not long after publishing *La luna e i falò* (*The Moon and the Bonfires*), the masterpiece which he felt encapsulated all that he had done before.

Between 1938 and 1949, Pavese wrote a series of short novels mostly set in Piedmont, either in the hills of the Langhe region or in Turin. These were all characterized by an economic narrative style combined with an intensively evocative sense of place, sharp and suggestive characterization, and a concrete colloquial-seeming language, inspired by recent American fiction, that brilliantly overcame the limitations of traditional literary prose. His progression, as he saw it, from conventional realism to what he called 'symbolic reality' is traceable in the critical essays he wrote from the mid-1930s onwards and in his literary diary, published posthumously as *Il mestiere di vivere* (*The Business of Living*). Here he develops a dualistic philosophical outlook that broadly echoes Leopardi, though he draws his specific concepts more from modern anthropology. As individuals and as a race, human beings are, he argues, irreconcilably split. First comes their primitive, savage side, the childhood self which remains in the adult as the source of all emotional and imaginative life; then there develops the rational, civilized side, which tends inevitably to suppress and deaden the other, but which can only be denied at the cost of denying an essential aspect of humanity. The task we face is at best to maintain a precarious balance between these two opposed parts of our being. Literature does not enable us necessarily to achieve this balance in our lives, but it offers, through what Pavese calls symbols, the means of exploring and gaining awareness of the fundamental elements of our nature.

How symbols work is the underlying subject of *La luna e i falò*, which as realist narrative is little more than the account of a Piedmontese émigré's return visit from America to the rural Langhe in which he grew up, conversations about the past with old friends and acquaintances being interspersed with his own memories of his early years and of the United States. But the thematic centre of the novel is a series of oppositions: between the Piedmontese hills and the sea, Italy and America, the countryside and the city, childhood and adulthood, the primitive and the civilized, feeling and reason. The personal story of Anguilla, the protagonist and narrator, named after the eel that returns to the river in which it is born, is a journey that takes him from the first element in all these oppositions to the second, from the Langhe to Genoa, the sea, America, and then back to where he started. The hills and countryside of his childhood embody the primitive state of emotional and imaginative union with the world that constitutes the childhood experience of everyone, and also the essential condition of savage peoples. In moving to the city and the sea, Anguilla retraces every individual's, and the human race's, development from this primitive state to a condition of rational awareness, the effect of which is to detach the individual or the race from its former condition. Almost all the people associated with Anguilla's childhood have departed or are dead, a point underlined in the climactic final pages of the novel, which describe with deliberately mythic overtones the execution by the partisans of the young, beautiful, and perfidious Santa and the subsequent burning of her body. Like all humanity, Anguilla is destined to be irresistibly drawn back to the source of his entire emotional and imaginative life, only to find himself excluded from it. As he cannot decide where he really belongs, in the country or the city, in the hills or on the sea, so the human race is inevitably divided between its primitive and civilized sides.

La luna e i falò is remarkable in the way in which, in the space of a short novel, its 'symbolic reality', as Pavese termed it, works to fuse together such wide-ranging themes with more specific and personal ones. Anguilla is a symbolic Everyman only up to a point. A contrast runs through the novel between him and his friend Nuto – a carpenter who has stayed in the village, a former musician who used to play the clarinet at the local festivals, a believer in the local myths of the moon and the bonfires of the book's title, and either a communist or a communist sympathizer who thinks rural society must be changed. Anguilla has had quite different experiences and has a quite different outlook. Fundamentally, he remains the foundling, the bastard outsider, that he always was. Symbolically, he is close to representing the intellectual outsider that Pavese always felt himself to be, in spite of his attempts to engage politically in the immediate aftermath of the war.

Pavese's form of theoretical reflection is very much of his time, and, as with the other authors we have considered, proceeds in tandem with his creative work. This is not always the rule with more recent writers. Umberto Eco published his first novel, *Il nome della rosa (The Name of the Rose)*, in 1980 at a relatively late stage in his career, when he already had an international reputation in the fields of literary theory and semiotics (the general theory of signs), as well as a national reputation in Italy as a cultural journalist and essayist. His *Opera aperta* (*The Open Work*, 1962) had provided the most robust and interesting theoretical support behind the neo-avant-garde of the 1960s. *Il nome della rosa* and its successor, *Il pendolo di Foucault* (*The Foucault Pendulum*, 1988), represent in different ways the broad theoretical interests and principles of *Opera aperta*, as these had subsequently been elaborated by Eco into a full theory of semiotics.

One of the central tenets of Eco's semiotic theory is that the meaning of signs, including language, can be understood only by reference to other signs, never to things in the 'real' world. The rose of the first novel's title refers to a Latin verse, quoted at the end, which says precisely this: names are all that we possess of reality. Our knowledge of reality is also fundamentally disordered: the world of signs is a labyrinth through which there is no single path, in which there is an infinite variety of possible connections. This central tenet of Eco's semiotics contrasts with the stable, ordered world of the monastery in which the story of serial murder and detection is set. The library in particular represents the intellectual order of the books it contains and of the religious community it serves; it is also a sort of labyrinth or maze, but one with a single path through it to the truth. At the end of the novel, the library is burnt down, anticipating, metaphorically, the final destruction of this medieval world, already seriously threatened, as the characters repeatedly observe, by the new culture of the cities and their secular universities.

Eco's Holmes-like detective William of Baskerville seems to represent the modern world which replaces that of the monastery, displaying a striking acquaintance with semiotic theory and, unlike his pupil Adso (the Watson figure) and the rest of the characters in the book, recognizing that there is no single path through the labyrinth of knowledge: he shares Eco's idea of the essentially unknowable nature of things and of the provisional, hypothetical nature of the structures we find in them. This view is confirmed for him by his discovery, at the end of the book, that the series of murders was not the product of a single design drawn, as he had supposed, from the book of the Apocalypse, but was in large part determined by chance; his mistake had been to pursue a 'semblance of order', when he should have known that 'there is no order in the universe'. His response is not, however, to despair, but to affirm the broad intellectual and political values that have governed Eco's work from *Opera aperta* onwards. Confronted by the conflicting political interests of a savagely oppressive Papacy and an equally narrow and intolerant Franciscan opposition, William's attitude is to agree with neither side, but to see right and wrong in both, to make distinctions where others confuse issues and see similarities where others see utter difference. Like Eco, he is a doubter by principle who believes in democracy rather than oppression and in discussion rather than revelation, all in accordance with his theoretical recognition of the impossibility of certain knowledge.

Il nome della rosa, and Eco's work as a whole, show how the two tendencies we outlined at the end of Chapter 1 can co-exist to impressive effect in a single writer: the tendency to withdraw into the world of literature and abstract ideas, and the tendency to engage in the world of concrete reality. The theory that underlies Eco's novel is integrally bound up with his thinking about political issues and the writer's social responsibilities. In the next chapter, we shall turn to the strong political element that runs through the whole of Italian literature from the Middle Ages to the present day, reflecting the country's long history of conflict and disunity. Few writers follow the example of Dante in promoting specific political programmes or parties, but a great many, obliquely or directly, make contemporary political problems and issues the subject of their work. We shall also see more examples of the mediation of these concerns through the prism of abstract theorization, as well as some strikingly original ways of making politics the subject of literature.

Chapter 4
Politics

Non fu sul campo che morirono i suoi Gracchi – mi disse

['It wasn't on the battlefield that her Gracchi died,' she said]
(Vittorini)

Elio Vittorini wrote *Conversazione in Sicilia* (*Conversation in Sicily*) in Florence in (probably) 1937, when the Fascist regime had been in power for a decade and a half, and still had a wide base of popular support. He himself had been an enthusiastic 'left-wing' Fascist, seeing the corporate state as a radical means to social and economic change. In the face of the regime's real allegiances, he had argued that Italy should intervene on the Republican side in the Spanish Civil War. Mussolini's active support for General Franco's Nationalists, together with the Fascist regime's failure to bring about the social revolution it kept declaring was under way, led Vittorini to have serious doubts about Fascism and move hesitantly towards Communism. But it was only in 1943 that he became actively involved in the Communist resistance in Milan.

Conversazione in Sicilia is a political novel, but any anti-Fascism is concealed or coded. Vittorini had no difficulty publishing the book in 1938, and subsequent editions followed during the war years. Reviews, which appeared in the principal Fascist papers

8. Elio Vittorini (right) with Alberto Moravia in the 1950s

and magazines, were generally favourable. If there were doubts, they were about the way the story is told. The narrative tends towards the lyrical and metaphorical, and the dialogue is stylized, deliberately repetitive, with an almost liturgical air: Vittorini himself later said it was more like opera. As the narrative progresses, it makes increasing use of symbolic and fantastical elements, particularly in the concluding chapters, which oust completely the tenuous realism of the opening. At the same time, the novel keeps coming back with ever greater insistence to the need for change, perhaps even revolutionary change, in individuals and politics. Vittorini's use of modernist techniques to explore a personal and political crisis has enabled the novel to remain as rich and powerful as it ever was, yet it also points to the way in which it was always at one remove from political actuality.

Like Vittorini, the narrator and protagonist is a Sicilian, Silvestro, living and working in the north, who recounts a journey in which, in a state of depressed indifference and

astratti furori (abstract furies), he leaves a bleak and wet
Milan to visit his mother in Sicily. Most of the book consists of
conversations with the characters encountered first on the train
going south and then in Sicily, where he travels on to his mother's
cold, sunny village in the 'pure heart' of the island. The journey is
both external and internal, material and moral, a 'journey in the
fourth dimension', as the narrator calls it. It is a process of inner
awakening, the revival of the ability to respond and feel, and also
one of progressive understanding. Silvestro learns from each of
the emblematic characters he speaks with, and then moves on to
learn something from the next, as the 'wheel of the journey' stops
and restarts. The reunion with his mother brings back childhood
memories, and also his ability to respond to the world around
him, in both its good and bad aspects. This raises the central
question of the book: how does one retain the clarity of feeling,
the 'certainty' that belongs to childhood, in the face of the
extreme poverty and suffering of the *mondo offeso*, the offended
or outraged world. His mother's attitude of gruff practical charity
is one answer, but plainly an inadequate one. So too is that of his
companions in the next stage of the journey, who, in the course of
an extended drinking bout in a cave-like tavern at the top of the
village, both celebrate the beauties of the world and lament the
offences that blight it. This act of lyrical effusion (Vittorini later
associated drunkenness with 'subjectivity as an end in itself')
also leaves Silvestro dissatisfied, and is in turn superseded by an
encounter with the ghost of his brother, a soldier who has
recently died on the battlefield fighting, we may assume, with the
troops that Mussolini sent to Spain to support Franco against the
republicans. When the next morning the whole chorus of Sicilian
characters assembles, the issue is now death in battle: to their
question 'Is it much to suffer?', the dead man, speaking more
within Silvestro than to the others, can only reply with an
enigmatic 'Ehm'. Silvestro has recovered his capacity to feel
and respond emotionally and imaginatively, and can see that
something needs to be done for the *mondo offeso*. It is the next
and final stage that is problematic, as the 'Ehm' seems to suggest.

Action may result in pain and death, and it may be misguided. The novel ends in a final dialogue with the mother, whom he had compared to the Roman matron Cornelia, whose sons, the brothers Gracchi (both tribunes of the people), died for their country. She has now discovered the truth: as she says in the line at the head of this chapter, it wasn't on the battlefield that the Gracchi died. Vittorini's hard-won conclusion, we may deduce, is that a full inner life is not sufficient in itself, but must be accompanied by the kind of political commitment exemplified by the Gracchi, who were murdered because of their efforts at social reform. Yet the allusive classical formulation points away from the immediate political arena towards a kind of literary exclusiveness, a fertile ambivalence which recurs repeatedly in Vittorini, and which characterizes the whole tradition of political literature in Italy.

Conversazione in Sicilia was written quite early in Vittorini's career, but he rightly felt that it contained the core of all his work. He was a restless innovator, and the two main novels that followed appear strikingly different from *Conversazione* and from each other, yet they circle around the same issues. The first, *Uomini e no* (*Men and Not Men*), was written in secret in 1944–5 in Milan during the Resistance against the Nazis and Mussolini's Salò Republic. It uses stylized repetition, and the alternation of narrative with lyrical, ostensibly authorial, reflection, to articulate a complex but deeply felt expression of Resistance ideology, and for that reason was a success with ex-partisans when it was published after the war.

The second novel was written shortly afterwards and is as oblique as its title, *Il Sempione strizza l'occhio al Frejus* (*The Simplon [Tunnel] Winks at the Fréjus [Tunnel]*). The ostensible subject is poverty in post-war Milan, but the narrative becomes an allegory of the relationship between the writer and the working class, and its moral seems to be that the only basis for progress in the future is an imaginative appreciation of the working class's past history, symbolized in the image of the elephant and picked up in the title of the English translation, *The Twilight of the Elephant*. The theme of the writer-as-intellectual, as mentioned in the previous chapter, is particularly strong here, but runs throughout Vittorini's career, in his case as an intellectual of a very public kind.

Throughout the post-war decades up to his death in 1966, he was at least as important as a cultural journalist and literary impresario as he was as a novelist. When most writers of any note, including himself, were members of the Communist Party, he took on the party secretary, Palmiro Togliatti, and made the case for a committed literature which was not simply voicing the party line but which remained true to itself as literature. It was probably the saving grace of Italian writing of the time. Vittorini then moved on, keeping his fundamental perspective as it had been, but constantly attempting to deal with new possibilities and dilemmas, from the impact of industrialization to the new French novel. His *Diario in pubblico* (*Diary in Public*, 1957), an anthology that he made of his reviews and articles, is both an autobiography and an account of Italian culture from the 1930s to the mid-1950s.

* * *

How to bring politics and literature into alignment, and how to reconcile the political and the ethical, have been recurrent questions in Italian literature, always against a backdrop of classical reference and thought. Perhaps surprisingly, *Conversazione in Sicilia* is closer to Dante than to the American authors such as Hemingway whom Vittorini admired. Silvestro's journey echoes that of the *Divine Comedy*, an exemplary physical journey that is also a journey of the mind. Vittorini's vision of moral progress, political enlightenment, and self-fulfilment as inseparable from each other is fundamentally akin to Dante's conviction, shared with a long tradition of thought going back to Aristotle, that the same essential standards apply to the life of individuals and to the government of states: the ruler's task is primarily to enable people to live their lives virtuously, that is, to realize the potential for virtue which is an essential part of their human nature.

The *Divine Comedy* starts from the conviction that the contemporary world is morally corrupt and that Dante and all his fellow men are on the road to damnation. Divided into three *cantiche* and a hundred cantos, it begins with the account of Dante the character's frustrated attempt to escape from the dark wood that represents his own state of sin; the way towards virtue is blocked by three beasts, of which the third, the wolf apparently representing avarice, is cast as the most dangerous. Rescued from the wolf by the soul of the Roman poet Virgil, sent by his dead beloved Beatrice, Dante is taken on an exceptional personal journey: first through the ten circles of Hell; then up the mountain of Purgatory to the Earthly Paradise, where at last he meets Beatrice; then, with Beatrice replacing Virgil as his guide, up through the heavens, until he reaches the true seat of the blessed, and at the very end of the poem has a vision of God himself. It is a journey of individual salvation, grounded in Dante's own personal history, and above all in his love of Beatrice, but the personal continually merges with or exemplifies universal issues. As well as being strongly individual characters, Virgil and Beatrice represent and voice general moral and political truths, just as Dante the character is in essential ways an Everyman in spite of the exceptional privilege granted to him.

Again and again, the poem turns to the corruption and disorder of the world, the prime source of which is avarice or human greed, though the emphasis changes as the journey progresses. In *Inferno*, the souls Dante meets retain a great deal of their worldly selves. They speak compulsively about their lives on earth, and embody in intensified form their earthly vices and, in some cases, their earthly virtues as well. The punishments that they undergo are not so much vindictive or retaliatory, still less sadistic, as metaphorical representations of the spiritual condition they have put themselves in through the sins that they have committed. For

Dante, there is always the possibility until the very moment of death of gaining freedom from the past through repentance, but in Hell, as in the world above, this has not happened. It is thus that *Inferno* acts as an immediate, concrete representation of the world above, a graphic reinforcement of what is said in the poem's recurrent diatribes about its state.

Inferno thus shows the world as it is, but with few explanations of the reasons why it is in such a state. *Purgatorio*, the second *cantica*, is the realm where repentant souls undergo purification in order to prepare themselves for Paradise, and where Dante is himself morally purified. This process includes a cleansing of the rational faculties, which brings with it a greater understanding of the nature of man and the world. In the exact middle of the *cantica*, and of the *Comedy* as a whole, the soul of a Lombard knight, identified only as Marco, explains that the corruption of the world is primarily due to the Papacy's assumption of powers that belong to the Holy Roman Empire. The two institutions were set up by Divine Providence to lead human beings to their proper ends, as separate and complementary guides, and the Pope should concern himself only with spiritual matters, leaving all earthly power and possessions to the Emperor. It is an argument that Dante elaborates later in detailed philosophical terms in the *Monarchia*, the polemical treatise on government by a supreme single ruler (the monarch) that he is now thought to have written in the last year or two of his life. The argument is also represented allegorically in the general lines of the journey of the *Comedy*: Virgil leads Dante to the Earthly Paradise as the Emperor should lead men to happiness on earth; Beatrice leads him to the Heavenly Paradise in the highest heaven, the Empyrean, as the Pope and Church should lead men to heavenly happiness in the life to come. It is given more concentrated and forceful figurative expression at the end of *Purgatorio*, where in a pageant representing the whole of human history, Dante sees the Church become a monster, the Papacy a whore, and the French monarchy (which has abused its powers by moving the Papacy from Rome to Avignon in 1305) a giant.

9. Dante and the simoniac Popes. Manuscript illustration of Dante's encounter in hell (*Inferno* XIX) with the Popes who used their office for financial gain

For Dante, the Church is not the sole problem. There is also the weakness and corruption of secular rulers, and the human greed that shows itself in the rampant commercialism of contemporary society, a major force for social disorder – a view which sets Dante in firm opposition to the economic development that fuelled the life of the medieval communes and laid the foundations for the Renaissance. But he can never let go of the idea that the Papacy is the main culprit. Near the end of *Paradiso*, St Peter delivers the most violent of the many diatribes on the subject in the *Comedy*: the Papacy is now vacant in the eyes of God, and a usurper Pope has turned Rome into a 'sewer of blood and stench' (27.25–6). At the same time, the political stance of the *Comedy* seems to develop with the world in which Dante was writing. Beatrice prophesies that the whore and the giant of the pageant will soon be dealt with by a mysterious figure she only identifies as a DXV, a Five

Hundred and Fifteen and also the anagram of *dux*, leader. Dante probably has in mind Henry VII of Luxemburg who became Holy Roman Emperor in 1308, and whose descent into Italy two years later he acclaimed as Italy's political salvation. By the time he was writing the greater part of *Paradiso*, however, Henry had died of malaria outside the walls of Pisa. Beatrice can only say in her last speech in canto 30 that Italy's blind greed made it unready for its providential leader.

Politics is thus not forgotten in *Paradiso*, but this last *cantica* of the poem moves well beyond *Purgatorio* by combining political polemic with a powerful assertion of the essential metaphysical order of the world, whatever the mess human beings have made of it. 'All things are ordered amongst themselves', says Beatrice in the first canto (ll. 103–5), 'and this is the form that makes the universe similar to God'. While the souls in *Inferno* represent contingent disorder and conflict, those in *Paradiso* represent this underlying divine order through their mutual harmony, illustrated through images of light, music, and dance. Doctrinal dissertations by Beatrice and other blessed souls on topics such as astral influences, free will, the Incarnation, and divine justice provide an intellectual correlative that Dante obviously sees as part of divine bliss, though post-Romantic readers may well find them taxing. Each of the dissertations adds to Dante the character's understanding of the fundamental problem of the relationship between man and God. Although Beatrice insists that the greater part of this is beyond human comprehension, the vision with which the poem concludes provides the answer. Seeing the 'universal form' of creation contained in the mind of God, followed by three conjoined circles representing the three persons of the Trinity, Dante struggles in a final effort to understand how the divine and the human are related in God the Son. He is rewarded with a lightning-flash of understanding, which overwhelms his rational faculties and his powers as a poet, but which is the fulfilment of his journey and the affirmation of the belief that everything does indeed cohere, including this multivalent, constantly evolving poem that he can now write for our benefit.

* * *

Dante's radical separation of the spiritual and secular authorities was unsustainable in the face of real political developments in his own time and for long after. Subsequent writers took a more earth-bound view. More than Dante, Petrarch served as a model in this respect, as he did for style and language. Always aware of the need to treat his powerful patrons with respect, but determined to establish an independence for himself as a writer, he regularly emphasized the benefits of withdrawal from the public and practical sphere into a life of study and reflection, the classical *otium*. On the other hand, he also fulminated against the corruption of the Papal court in Avignon, and for a while entertained the dangerous fantasy that the Roman politician Cola di Rienzo might resuscitate ancient Roman republicanism. In later life, he accepted and enthused over the Visconti of Milan and the Carrara of Padua in a way that his republican friends in Florence found hard to accept. The *Canzoniere* mostly excludes politics in favour of love, spiritual unease, and poetry, while also leaving a political window open with three strong political *canzoni* and three sonnets denouncing Avignon. Whether they wrote poetry or prose, in Italian or Latin, many of Petrarch's successors negotiated the same tricky path, taking advantage of the *otium* offered by absolute rulers, yet with an eye out for moments when it seemed possible that long-lost freedoms might be restored. Early 15th-century humanists revived Roman republican ideals of civic duty in the struggle between nominally republican Florence and the Milan of the Visconti. But the language of this so-called civic humanism was classical Latin, and in many ways rhetorical accomplishment was the message rather than ideological commitment; writers seem to have had little compunction switching between republicanism and monarchism as circumstances demanded.

The most original political outcome of the humanist revival emerges at the beginning of the 16th century with Niccolò Machiavelli, who gives the preceding debates about government a revolutionary turn by radically challenging the classical association of politics and ethics, dismissing Christian values as debilitating, treating the Church as a purely political entity, and combining the humanist study of the classical past with the practical lessons of contemporary history. His most extreme statements are in the *Principe* (*The Prince*, c. 1513), his short treatise on how to become sole ruler of a state and hold onto power once you have it. It rests on a concept of *virtù* as active ability, which can if necessary become ruthless and amoral, and is justified by Machiavelli through an appeal to the lesson of experience and history, that traditional ideas of goodness can have disastrous consequences for the governed and those who govern them. All this was enough to make Machiavelli Old Nick, the devil, in England, and the shock (which may have been calculated) has not quite dispersed even now, the more so since these fundamental ideas are only partly qualified elsewhere. His other major political work, the much longer *Discorsi* (*Discourses*, c. 1516) on the first ten books of Livy, is not so much a commentary on the ancient Roman historian as an enthusiastic celebration and analysis of the Roman republic, which Machiavelli regrets has few direct lessons for the corrupt age in which he lives. It is grounded in an appreciation of the robustness of Roman institutions and individuals, in other words, a more civic version of the *virtù* that he characterizes more succinctly and radically in the *Principe*. Florentine contemporaries do not appear to have been disturbed by any of this amorality, which is evident also in Machiavelli's comedies. The historian and political thinker Francesco Guicciardini, who was Machiavelli's social superior and had much more direct experience of actual government, was deeply critical, but mainly on the grounds that Machiavelli set too much store by Roman precedent and absolute rules. Neither, he declared, were guarantees of success in the real world. He was probably right, but it would be the incisive and striking

Machiavelli who would be read by Napoleon, not the prosaic Guicciardini.

The absolutism of the *Principe*, and the contrast with the more republican *Discorsi*, probably stem from Machiavelli's conviction of the need for strong political leadership in the face of the foreign irruptions into Italian affairs from the end of the 15th century. The ensuing turmoil and instability are also reflected in his acute sense of the unpredictability of events, personified in the figure of *fortuna*, with its correlative that a major requirement of political *virtù* is the ability to adapt to the ever-changing demands that she makes. The traumas of the time are discernible in the work of many other writers, including Machiavelli's two most illustrious contemporaries, Castiglione and Ariosto, whom we shall discuss in more detail in the next chapter. Both might appear to be concerned mostly with ideal or unreal worlds. But Castiglione puts a quite Machiavellian stress on the need for adaptation and dissimulation, as well as on the need for sound political guidance; and Ariosto's chivalric universe is ruled by chance, coincidence, and unpredictable magical forces that echo Machiavelli's *fortuna*, and that his knights, despite all their prowess, repeatedly fail to comprehend.

There is a long and distinguished tradition of Italian political thought following Machiavelli and Guicciardini, including names such as Paolo Sarpi, Pietro Giannone, and Cesare Beccaria. However, major literary works with significant political content do not appear again until the later 18th century. By then, Enlightenment ideas had taken hold in the north and in Naples, and the Risorgimento and Romanticism were both on the horizon. Giuseppe Parini satirized the idle nobility in *Il giorno* (1763), a mock heroic verse account with parallels to Pope of a day in the life of a young fop; in the next two decades, Vittorio Alfieri took political tyranny to task in his terse neo-classical tragedies; and, in the midst of the tumults that overwhelmed Europe after the French Revolution, Ugo Foscolo rewrote Goethe's *Werther* in *Le ultime lettere di Jacopo Ortis* (*The Last Letters of Jacopo Ortis*, 1802) as a despairing heroic lament, both for a failed love affair and for the extinction of the Venetian republic by Napoleonic Realpolitik. Just when the Austrian regime was restored after Napoleon's fall, the Romantic movement emerged as such in Milan, but its distinctively liberal political programme was as doomed as its programme for a popular literature, and some of the manifesto writers ended up in Austrian gaols. It was from this climate of reaction and defeat that the foremost Italian novelist of the century emerged.

* * *

Alessandro Manzoni was a product of the Milanese Enlightenment who became a Catholic convert and shared the aspirations of the Romantics, but who also took judicious stock of what it was possible to achieve in literature, given the political and cultural state of the country. Aside from his importance for Italian prose, his strength as a writer comes from blending classical, Enlightenment, and Romantic principles with his Christian beliefs, indeed from finding agreement between all of these. Professedly a Romantic, he shares few of the attitudes that characterized the Romantics of Northern Europe as well as his anti-Romantic contemporary Leopardi. Literature should be primarily concerned, he argued, to instil the traditional values of the good, the useful, and the true in its readers, and to this end he largely stripped *I promessi sposi* of what he considered distracting or immoral features such as adulterous passion, and instead attempted to integrate with his fictional inventions as much historical fact and analysis as the novel could bear. The truths that concerned him most were Christian ones, and the moral with which the novel ends is as explicit and didactic as his Romantic friends could wish: life is full of hardships which often cannot be avoided, but faith in God makes it possible to bear them and to benefit from them. But the novel has much more interesting things to say, even if Italian schoolrooms have often stopped at this point.

Set in Spanish-ruled 17th-century Lombardy, it is built around the story of the betrothed of the title, Renzo and Lucia, the first lower-class protagonists to be treated seriously in Italian literature, who go through the canonical trials of separation and exile before being finally reunited. The rosy picture of virtue rewarded is however set against a picture of chaos, abuse, and incompetence. The depiction of the governing classes cannot help but evoke the Austrian rule of Manzoni's own time, even if Manzoni suggests that the Spanish abuses were more brutal. Most of the novel conveys a strong sense of injustice, with a sharp contrast drawn between those who tyrannize and exploit, and those who fight for justice and the good of others. As a Christian, Manzoni wishes to believe that God's Providence is active in human history; as a student of history, he finds the evidence hard to discover. Its scope widening as it progresses, the novel's climax is a plague, the spread of which is started by human stupidity and ignorance, and which reduces Milan to hell on earth. Dante is very much in evidence in these pages, and the solution is similarly Dantesque. Rain comes and washes away the corruption infecting the material world: God has intervened. The problem is that he might not have. It is not history, but only faith and hope, that indicate that he might intervene again.

More positive notes are struck as the Risorgimento gathers force. The other great novel of the mid-19th century is much more explicitly political, and much more contemporary. Ippolito Nievo's *Confessioni di un italiano* (*Confessions of an Italian*, 1857–8) was written by an officer in Garibaldi's army of liberation who drowned at sea while still a young man, in the course of the 1860 campaign. His narrator, however, is an octogenarian, looking back on his earlier years, beginning with a boyhood in the lazy, idyllic rural world of the 18th-century Veneto. This is often felt to be the most appealing part of the novel, which then moves on to the active role the narrator plays in Venice as it is first liberated and then dominated by the French, the despair of Restoration, and thirty years later the revolutions of 1848. The switchback of political adventures is intertwined with the story of his love for his beautiful, passionate, contradictory, and wayward cousin Pisana. It is the novel of Risorgimento patriotism, rhetoric, passion, and all, which most vividly relives the events leading up to the actual war of Unification.

The political disillusionment that set in when Unification failed to deliver all the patriots had hoped for has its literary correlative in *verismo*, the Italian version of Zola's French naturalism. Whereas Zola was an avowed socialist, the *veristi* attempted to engage with the social and economic realities of the time from a socially conservative position. Giovanni Verga, the greatest of them, was the son of a modest Sicilian landowner who, determined to win fame and fortune as a writer in Florence and Milan, tried various types of fiction before writing the stories and the two novels for which he is now principally known. His earlier novels have conventional late-Romantic subjects, a narrow range of social interests, and a good deal of rhetorical sentimentality. In the late 1870s, he underwent a literary conversion (partly occasioned by reading Zola and other French naturalists), which led him to plan a sequence of five novels, each dealing with a different stratum of society, beginning with the lowest, and with a new, 'impersonal' narrative style, constructed from the viewpoint of his characters.

He completed only the first two novels in the series, *I Malavoglia* (1881), about a Sicilian fishing family of the same name (translated as *The House by the Medlar Tree*), and *Mastro-don Gesualdo* (1888), the life of a Sicilian mason (*mastro*) who makes himself into a successful property-owner and becomes a *don* by marrying into the aristocracy. In both novels, 'impersonality' produces far more complex and interesting effects than the detached objectivity that Verga claimed to aim at. There is no single narrative voice in *I Malavoglia*, rather a shadowy chorus of narrators, who speak in an Italian that recreates the idioms and phrasing of Sicilan dialect, and whose point of view often merges with that of the named characters, or becomes that of the local populace. The fishing family of the title generally stands for tradition, loyalty, honour, and a stoic acceptance of hardship, which the novel supplies in abundance. One son tries to break away, only to return a failure and a drunkard, while the rest of the villagers are almost all dominated by a ruthless pursuit of personal advantage and a spiteful scorn for others. Tradition, rebellion, materialism are three possible responses to the destructive power of nature, society, and the new Italian state; all, for different reasons, are found wanting. The only option Verga seems to envisage is sympathetic contemplation of tragic inevitability.

In *Mastro-don Gesualdo*, the move up the social scale leads to a more standard form of Italian and less in the way of contrasting viewpoints. Virtually all the characters are dominated by self-interest, but some are more honest about it than others. Gesualdo, who becomes by far the richest man in the town, works relentlessly and with almost heroic energy for his own gain, whereas the provincial nobility and middle classes, which he both competes with and wishes to join, succumb to the economic forces they cannot handle and decline into poverty. They do so in the midst of hypocrisy, self-delusion, and viciousness, whereas Gesualdo is straightforward and capable of kindness when his interests are not at stake. But he too ultimately gains nothing, dying alone and despised in his aristocratic son-in-law's palace. It is a bleak vision of life in general and of the social and political issues of the time, perhaps a reactionary one, certainly one that sees little amelioration to be achieved by the writer or by literature – in contrast with the active, left-oriented vision of the mid-20th-century writers who saw themselves as Verga's heirs.

* * *

The best-known political novel in the 20th century before *Conversazione in Sicilia* was written in exile by an Abruzzese Communist in the process of breaking with the Communist Party and espousing a form of Christian socialism. Ignazio Silone's *Fontamara* (1933) recounts in a deliberately plain, almost *faux-naïf*, style the growing political consciousness of the peasants of the Abruzzo mountain village of the title, as they are increasingly exploited and persecuted by the Fascist regime and its supporters. The hero Berardo dies in prison, but his fate helps his comrades to a greater sense of the need for collective resistance. First published in Switzerland in a German translation which was later translated into English and distributed to Italian prisoners of war, the novel shows beneath its surface a personal disquiet which becomes even more apparent in Silone's later novels. There is now some evidence that Silone was a Fascist double-agent. If that undermines his status as a voice of anti-Fascism (he was always more highly regarded abroad than in his own country even after the war), it makes his writing a more complex as well as more compromised response to the realities of Fascism.

While *Fontamara* is a kind of fable, the other well-known work about the south from these years is much more concrete and documentary. Carlo Levi's *Cristo si è fermato a Eboli* (*Christ Stopped at Eboli*) is an account of its author's experiences in the southern village to which he was sent as an internal exile in 1935–6, after being implicated in anti-Fascist activities in Turin. A cultured doctor, Levi is amazed and horrified by the poverty, squalor, and pagan ignorance of the peasants amongst whom he finds himself, but whose human qualities he comes to know and appreciate. The book is not so much a protest against Fascist oppression as a call for something to be done for the peasantry of the south. It was published after the war in 1945 and was one of the books, by southerners as well as outsiders like Levi, which brought the issue to the notice of the country as a whole.

The literature of the post-war years might do all it could to steer away from ideological propaganda, in line with Vittorini's position, to give voice to the moral values of the Resistance while remaining true to itself as literature. Yet the project of committed literature (*letteratura impegnata*) was an uncomfortable one, unsustainable in the face of Cold War realities, and the changes in Italian society as the old peasant and artisan culture yielded to industrialization and consumerism. The writer who most represents the travails of *impegno* and its eventual abandonment is Italo Calvino, for whom the Resistance was a moment of political awakening, as it was for many intellectuals of his generation. His first significant novel, *Il sentiero dei nidi di ragno* (*The Path to the Spiders' Nests*, 1947), is the imaginative story of a young boy's experiences of partisan life in the hills, with an explicit message grafted on towards the end, when a partisan Communist intellectual spells out the need for self-aware political commitment. Calvino left the Communist Party after the Russian suppression of the 1956 uprising in Hungary. In the next phase of his fiction, while politics is not forgotten and the general sympathy for the Left remains, fantastical, imaginative, and individual elements gain the upper hand.

This is particularly the case in the three novels he put together as *I nostri antenati* (*Our Ancestors*, 1952–9). The earliest, *Il visconte dimezzato* (*The Cloven Viscount*), is set in the 17th century, and is about an Italian nobleman who is split in two by a Turkish cannonball, but lives on in two separate selves, one good and one bad. The second, *Il barone rampante* (*The Baron in the Trees*), concerns another Italian nobleman, this time in the late 18th and early 19th centuries, who decides at an early age to live the rest of his life in the trees, without ever again touching the ground. The third, *Il cavaliere inesistente* (*The Non-Existent Knight*), relates the doings of a medieval knight in the army of Charlemagne, who consists of nothing but a mind enclosed in an empty suit of armour. Calvino indicated, in a later preface to the trilogy, that the first and the third are concerned with man's loss of human identity in the modern industrial and capitalist world, and that the second illustrates a solution to this loss of identity through self-affirmation, choosing a path of action and staying with it to the end. All this may be true, but the baron in the trees, as he appears in the novel, may also be read as an image of the ideal position of the writer or intellectual in the later 1950s – detached and aware, while still engaging with contemporary events. The hopes of making a direct contribution to social and political change have evaporated and any representation of contemporary reality is at best indirect. Characteristically, Calvino sees the writer's political commitment as consisting in the very general representation of the difficulty of living in the modern world, a lack of specificity that recalls that of his mentor Vittorini. In his later fiction, he steps back still further, concerning himself principally with issues of perception and understanding, and the various semiotic systems, including literary ones, which shape the world in which we live.

The 1950s and 1960s were the heyday of the Italian political novel. The partisan novel, largely stripped of problems of *impegno*, shows a new vitality in Luigi Meneghello's autobiographical *I piccoli maestri* (*The Minor Masters*, 1964), and perhaps most remarkably in Beppe Fenoglio's *Il partigiano Johnny* (*Johnny the Partisan*), published in 1968 five years after his death and written in an odd mixture of English and Italian in line with its hero's, and author's, Anglophile interests. Politics become more explicitly polemical in Leonardo Sciascia's work about the Mafia and political corruption, in Sicily but also in Italy and, by implication, in the world at large. *Il giorno della civetta* (*The Day of the Owl*, 1961) and *A ciascuno il suo* (*To Each His Own*, 1966) are evocative and compelling accounts of organized crime in small Sicilian towns and its connection with political powers at both national and regional level. Sciascia called this connection a 'concatenation', a topic that he treated in a rather more allegorical vein in *Il contesto* (*Equal Danger*, 1971), set in a fictitious country that seems partly Sicilian, party generically Mediterranean, and partly South American. All three novels end with the failure or death of their protagonists, who find that they cannot make sense of the evil in which they become embroiled.

Italian intellectuals as a whole were becoming as aware as Calvino that *impegno* was increasingly a tired slogan or an impossibility. 'Have you made your ideological choice?' asks a threatening phantom in one of the poems of Vittorio Sereni, and the answer, which author after author also gave, is in effect, no, in spite of my best efforts, but I can't stop trying to do so. One way of breaking the stalemate was proposed by the neo-avant-garde Gruppo 63, named after the year when it was founded, of which Eco was the theorist and which equated experimental art, and especially experimental poetry, with revolution, taking the Communist Party to task for its conformism and by now ritual veneration of the Resistance. In an interesting postscript to this argument, Eco observed a few years later that it was soon to be overtaken by events. When in 1968 it looked as if the revolution was actually going to happen, as the workers and students took to the streets in Italy and across Europe, the idea of any form of literature, experimental or not, having a political thrust became less and less convincing. Antonio Tabucchi is symptomatic: his ambiguous, often mysterious fictions repeatedly raise the problem of getting political issues into some sort of focus; he is at his clearest in *Sostiene Pereira* (*Pereira Maintains*, 1994), the story of a middle-aged journalist coming round to a modest form of anti-Fascism, which however is set in 1930s Lisbon, not contemporary Italy. There are of course exceptions. Dario Fo, who belongs to the same generation as Calvino, continued his unique brand of left-wing political theatre after his receipt of the Nobel Prize in 1997, now taking the Berlusconi regime as his target. More recently, detective fiction has been used to highlight political and institutional corruption. But the most disturbing visions of early 21st-century Italian society have emerged from accounts of their experiences by North African migrants, and the dramatic and courageous exposure of the Neapolitan Camorra in Roberto Saviano's *Gomorra* (2006).

The next chapter continues in broader terms the theme of engagement with reality. Italy is a Catholic country, and over the centuries a great deal has been written in Italian on religious issues. Yet Italian writers across the centuries, from Dante onwards, show a striking inclination to concentrate on this world rather than the next, generally tending towards secular attitudes and sometimes expressing strong moral criticism of the Catholic Church. This secularism may not in itself be remarkable in writers of the modern age, but it is already apparent in the Middle Ages and Renaissance, encouraged by the fact that many communes and *signorie* found themselves, at one time or another, at war with the Papacy. Until Unification, the Papacy remained a political force of a conservative, repressive, and frequently aggressive kind: hence the strongly anticlerical bias of the Risorgimento and the new Italian state, only resolved by the Concordat of 1929. Even after that, intellectuals remained mostly indifferent or hostile to the Church; for many, the gap was widened by the decades of right-wing Catholic government after the war. As we shall see, from the Renaissance onwards this secularism has also had a strongly pessimistic bias, the prime reason for which we can again identify in the country's difficult history.

Chapter 5
Secularism

La vita non è né bella né brutta, ma è originale

[Life is neither good nor bad, but it's original]

(Svevo)

In 1922 in Trieste, the principal Mediterranean port of the Austro-Hungarian Empire until the end of World War I, a secularized Italian-speaking Jewish businessman named Ettore Schmitz published his third novel twenty years after the failure of his second, during which time he had more or less resigned himself to a career in commerce. Maybe this novel too would have sunk without trace, if Schmitz had not been a friend of James Joyce and if it hadn't been singled out in a review by the young Eugenio Montale. As it was, in the unpredictable chancy way the novel itself saw as characteristic of human life, *La coscienza di Zeno* was quickly picked on as a masterpiece by up-to-date readers, and its author became famous as Italo Svevo, the pseudonym in which Schmitz emblematically brought together the Italian (Italo) and Germanic (Svevo from Swabia in Germany) aspects of the culture of his city. Svevo, aged sixty-three in 1922, delighted in his success, but chance had not finished with him: he died five years later in a car accident, with only the opening chapters of a follow-up completed.

10. Italo Svevo smoking. Svevo himself was as avid a smoker as the protagonist of *La coscienza di Zeno*

La coscienza di Zeno begins with the narrator Zeno's long account of his unsuccessful attempts to give up smoking, and ends with a prediction of the destruction of the natural environment and eventually of the world. The chapters in between narrate retrospectively, in roughly chronological order, the death of his father, his marriage, an extra-marital affair, and the disastrous business enterprise of his brother-in-law. Deeply ironic and paradoxical, with frequent moments of high comedy, the main narrative is ostensibly written by Zeno for Dr S., his psychoanalyst, with a view to curing an indeterminate sickness that Zeno believes has blighted his life. The final chapter jumps forward in time to World War I and switches to diary form, in the course of which Zeno announces that he has abandoned psychoanalysis and is finally cured, his health being due not to some spiritual or psychological renewal but to success as a war profiteer. Svevo's father-in-law's firm, for which he worked, sold marine paint to the navies of both sides during the war, and Zeno does something comparable. It is immediately after this unsettling turnaround that Zeno makes his prediction of global destruction, disconcerting the reader even more with the shift of tone and scope, and underlining the profoundly serious and pessimistic vision behind the irony and the comedy.

Against the background of a realistic narrative tradition that tended to concentrate on the big events in life, the opening chapter on smoking marked a polemical shift of attention towards the comedy of everyday issues and the psychological complexities that surround them. Throughout the events narrated in subsequent chapters, the predominant focus remains on Zeno's inner concerns, intentions, and reactions. On the one hand, there is his *coscienza*, the Italian word embracing 'consciousness' in general as well as 'conscience', and on the other, his relationship with the world around him. Perpetually engaged in the search for an illusory sense of health and in a struggle for supremacy acted out in the trivial interchanges of ordinary life, he can rarely translate his egotistical intentions into effect. Either inner conflicts get in the way, or his actions and behaviour are interpreted quite differently by those around him, or life itself turns out in a way that he does not expect. The story of his marriage is exemplary. He desperately seeks the hand of the beautiful and 'healthy' Ada, but is indignantly rejected by her. In order (he says) to ensure himself a good night's sleep, he proposes instead to her beautiful younger sister Alberta. Turned down in a rather more kindly way, he proposes to the next, much plainer sister Augusta, for whom he feels little attraction, but who accepts.

The marriage turns out to be wholly successful. Zeno feels surrounded by love and enjoys a well-being he acknowledges he could never have had with Ada, who in contrast falls sick and loses all her beauty: he was like an archer who hits the bulls-eye on a target, he says, but the target next to the one he was aiming at. His father-in-law, whom he also much admired for his 'healthy' success as a businessman, falls ill as well, while his brother-in-law Guido, the successful rival for the healthy Ada's hand, turns out to be a business disaster, ruins himself, and commits suicide, though not, it seems, intentionally. The 'sick' Zeno eventually saves Ada's family fortune as a result of a winning streak on the stock-market. Life seems indeed to be neither good nor bad but original, as Zeno observes in the quotation at the head of this chapter. He continues with a comment that expresses the heart of the book's vision:

> Simply recalling everything we humans expected from life was enough for us to see how strange it was, and to reach the conclusion that mankind is perhaps located in the midst of it by mistake and doesn't belong there.

Picking up the Darwinian maxim of the survival of the fittest that influenced so much contemporary thinking, Zeno sees the healthy as those who act without reflection in order to survive and triumph in the struggle for existence, and the sick as those who exercise their minds too much. The information received from an acquaintance, that every movement of the leg involves thirty-nine muscles, gives him a chronic limp. Thought is an impediment to successful action, though as the novel progresses the opposition between health and sickness is gradually reversed: sickness comes to be seen more as a universal condition, and not without its advantages over apparent health. What may matter more is the unconscious, and here Svevo draws enthusiastically on the then novel ideas of Sigmund Freud, though almost always ironically or comically. Social humiliation by his future brother-in-law leaves Zeno with a stabbing pain in his side, which recurs for much of his life at inappropriate moments; the lapse of going to the wrong funeral when his brother-in-law dies may be deliberate; Dr S. is a parody of an analyst; and so on. Some critics have argued that Svevo has created in Zeno one of those clever patients who use their knowledge of Freud as a defence mechanism against the psychoanalysis that they want and reject at the same time. However, the novel leaves the reader free to accept or reject Freudian explanations. What does seem clear is the deep-rooted pessimism about the possibilities of the human mind really understanding either itself or life as a whole, though it is a pessimism which (up to that last chapter) is remarkably cheerful and resilient.

Svevo was almost an exact contemporary of Pirandello, and there are striking parallels between them. Unlike the Fascist Pirandello, Svevo was more of a Socialist, but in spite of the tumultuous events through which they lived, neither made political or social issues a central focus of their work. Instead, both articulate a deeply negative vision of the human mind and its relation to an unstable reality, couched mostly in terms of opposites – health and sickness in Svevo, life and form in Pirandello. Neither finds much of a way out, either rationally or in any other terms. Svevo is untouched by Judaism as a religion or set of beliefs, even if his cast of mind and cultural formation has something in common with other modern Jewish writers from Central Europe, such as Kafka or even Freud himself. Pirandello occasionally suggests benefits in a semi-mystical immersion in life without the attempt to give form to it, and his last plays attempt rather opaquely to propose mythic vision as a substitute for rationality. But both remain essentially secular in their outlook, unconsoled by anything except their humour and their art.

* * *

Secularism in Italian literature pre-dates by a long way the impact of Freud and Darwin on Christian thinking and belief, often with a pessimistic colouring that anticipates that of Svevo and Pirandello. In the 19th century, Manzoni's Catholic faith is exceptional for a major author, and contrasts with the atheism of the two greatest poets of Italian Romanticism. Foscolo's *Dei sepolcri* is a lyrical reflection on cemeteries published in 1807, inspired by a Napoleonic edict that the dead should be buried outside cities and therefore, in Foscolo's eyes, outside human society. It sees respect and affection for the dead as the one valid source of moral and imaginative vitality in human life, which otherwise is at the mercy of blindly mechanistic forces of creation and destruction. As we have seen, Leopardi's materialism is even harsher. Both poets seemed to struggle through to a heroically bleak vision, which resonated with the strongly anticlerical thrust of the Risorgimento patriots determined to wrest political power from the Church. Nievo, Verga, and many other 19th-century novelists followed an equally secular path.

But the secularism of Italian writers, and with it suspicion and hostility towards the political actions of the Papacy and the Church, goes back much further still, even if they co-exist with varying degrees of orthodox belief and practice. Dante is the signal, though rather exceptional, example. He found in Aristotle the principle, fundamental to ancient philosophy, that the goal of life is achieved through the exercise of human reason, since reason is mankind's peculiar property. The argument of the *Comedy* and the *Monarchia* (partly also present in the earlier *Convivio*), that men should be led to earthly happiness by the Roman Emperor and to heavenly happiness by the Pope, rests on the acceptance of the happiness of this life as an end in itself. This happiness consists in the pursuit of virtue and knowledge through rational action or speculation, in accordance with the precepts of Aristotle; happiness of the next life is achieved through the exercise of the Christian virtues of faith, hope, and charity on the basis of the authority of the scriptures. Relegating the primary relevance of Christianity to the next life, and arguing that life on earth should be governed entirely by reason and philosophy, is on the face of it a radically secular position. Quite how the two ends of life should be pursued on a day-to-day basis is not explained, however, the distinction being theoretical rather than practical: in one way or another, it seems, humans should pursue both goals simultaneously. It has indeed been argued that there are two Dantes, the secular, classical Dante and the religious one, and that much of the fascination of his work lies in the tension between them. This is one way of accounting for the moving prominence that Dante gives, in *Inferno*, to some of the damned souls: though condemned to eternal punishment, Francesca, Farinata, Brunetto Latini, Pier delle Vigne, Ulysses, Ugolino all display admirable or touching human qualities. The secular Dante is able to value these qualities, particularly those associated with the civic life and the pursuit of knowledge, at the same time as the religious Dante condemns the individuals that possess them because they were also sinners and refused the recourse to Divine Grace.

Qualified though it is, Dante's secularism looks forward to the humanist movement that began in his own lifetime and reached maturity in the early 15th century, some hundred years later, after his death. The humanists not only studied and taught classical languages and culture; they also assimilated the essentially worldly attitudes and principles of classical writers, making them the basis of their own writings on history and politics, morality and education. Fourteenth-century humanists were generally cautious in the way they promoted their classical interests, and were concerned to justify them in the face of possible religious objections. Petrarch, who led the classical revival, claimed rather defensively that classical literature in one way or another supported Christian teaching. The case of his friend and fellow humanist Boccaccio, to whom we shall return in the next chapter, is more complex. The *Decameron* is strongly anticlerical, and in spite of various assertions of conventional piety, is far more worldly than Dante ever is, not least because a high proportion of its hundred stories condone adulterous sexual desire in both men and women, and celebrate the practical intelligence they show in its pursuit. However, Boccaccio's other works in Italian stay closer to medieval conventions. His vernacular treatise in praise of Dante includes regretful criticism of the poet for excessive involvement in worldly affairs, for pride and lust, and for getting married.

In contrast, the most prominent humanists of the first half of the 15th century espoused classical values with a remarkable lack of reservation about their potential conflict with Christian doctrine. Humanist writers on education, such as Pierpaolo Vergerio, Leonardo Bruni, Leon Battista Alberti, and Enea Silvio Piccolomini (later Pope Pius II), give only limited space to religious observance, as something required of young people, and not a major part, sometimes not a part at all, of a curriculum which consisted almost exclusively in the systematic study of the ancients. In general, the purpose of a classical education is expressed in terms of worldly advantage and rational self-fulfilment: the Ciceronian concept of the *studia humanitatis* (the 'studies of humanity'), much cited by the educators and from which the term 'humanist' derives, rests on the principle that study makes man more human because it develops the intellect. If we can judge educational practice by these writings, the social elite that went through humanist schools not only learned to write good classical Latin and Greek, but became thoroughly immersed in the culture of the ancient world and received little instruction in the Christian religion.

Like Cicero and Dante, humanists of the earlier 15th century were also inclined to celebrate the life of active involvement in worldly affairs. Later 15th-century humanism takes a more metaphysical turn. Marsilio Ficino, who was a cleric, works from the comfortable assumption that Platonism and Christianity are fundamentally in agreement. His extensive writings include a Latin commentary on Plato's *Symposium*, the *De Amore* (*On Love*), which restates the Platonic conviction that the contemplation of God, the Supreme Good, is achievable purely through rational thought, not Divine Grace. Religious feeling and belief in the Catholic sense seem to take second place. Ficino was the intellectual mentor of the circle around Lorenzo de' Medici in Florence, though by no means a dictatorial one. His ideas make themselves felt in the religious and intellectual parts of Lorenzo's own vernacular verse, for instance, but Lorenzo also ranges into pastoral, comic, and other modes. In the most brilliant scholar and poet of the circle, Angelo Poliziano, Neoplatonism becomes at most a question of sensibility, not of ideas. His most substantial vernacular poem, the unfinished *Stanze per la giostra* (1475–8), celebrated a joust featuring Lorenzo's brother Giuliano, and was abandoned when Giuliano was murdered. It has been seen as Neoplatonic allegory, but it is above all a dazzling celebration of refined but sensuous earthly beauty, in Nature and in Giuliano's beloved Simonetta: the emphasis remains firmly on this world.

* * *

This implicit secularism will be re-affirmed much more strongly in the three major vernacular writers of the early 16th century, Machiavelli, Castiglione, and Ariosto, all of whom brought humanist learning and habits of mind to bear on everything they wrote. We discussed Machiavelli, the least learned, and the most polemical, of the three, in the preceding chapter. We can now turn to Castiglione and Ariosto.

Baldesar Castiglione's *Il libro del cortegiano* (*The Book of the Courtier*, printed in 1528) is a dialogue divided into four books, each of them purporting to record a day's discussion at the court of Urbino on the subject of the ideal courtier – a dialogue which, with its evocation of a now vanished world of courtly refinement and harmony, has much richer literary dimensions than the Ciceronian models on which it is loosely based. The first two books deal with the intrinsic qualities of the courtier and how these may be put into effect, the third with the lady at court and her attributes, the fourth with the courtier's relationship to his prince and society, concluding with a celebration of the Neoplatonic ideal of love placed in the mouth of the literary theorist, poet, and future cardinal Pietro Bembo. A synthesis of writings on the subject by the historical Bembo and Ficino before him, this conclusion makes a moving, elegant, and cultured ending to the book, but is in no sense the logical conclusion of the wholly earthbound discussions that precede it. The key values that run through these represent a marriage of humanist concerns with courtly practice: the courtier must be chivalrous, exercise moderation, adapt to custom, and be learned in the *studia humanitatis*. He must also pursue excellence in everything he does, yet always conceal the effort with *sprezzatura*, a form of grace or simplicity that hides the art and effort that may underpin it. This combination of excellence with *sprezzatura* is Castiglione's distinctive twist to the humanist principle of rational self-fulfilment: the end of life becomes not so much the pursuit of knowledge and virtue as the development of any human qualities suited to the court, and that allow the courtier to demonstrate, with the appearance of effortlessness, his superiority over others.

There is also here the implicit recognition of a fundamental gap between appearance and reality that is one of the overriding themes of Ludovico Ariosto's contemporary *Orlando furioso*. This enormous but fast-moving, readable poem in 46 canti is complete in itself, but is cast as a continuation of the *Orlando innamorato*, the similarly large-scale poem which Boiardo, Ariosto's predecessor as a court poet in Ferrara, had broken off in 1494 in the face of the French invasion. The plot centres on the wars of the Emperor Charlemagne and his knights against a mixed host of Saracen invaders; its ultimate origins are in the 11th-century *Song of Roland*, Roland having become Orlando in Italy. There had been a number of popularizing 15th-century versions, which Boiardo had renovated by introducing elements of love, magic, and individual adventure associated with the parallel tradition of

11. Raphael's portrait of Castiglione. The author seems to embody in himself the figure of the perfect courtier

Arthurian romance: hence the 'Orlando in love' of Boiardo's title, which becomes with Ariosto 'Orlando mad through love'. But while Boiardo's epic romance is not much more than a celebration of love, chivalry, and adventure, Ariosto merges humanist reading and thought with the popular tradition and produces a deeply serious, if ironic and often comic, reflection on human desire, effort, and understanding.

The *Orlando furioso* begins with the defeat of Charlemagne's armies outside Paris, and the consequent dispersal of his main champions; it ends with the defeat of the last surviving Saracen champion at the hands of Ruggiero, the mythical progenitor of

Ariosto's patrons, the house of Este. In between, sub-plots are inserted in enormous profusion, recounting the adventures of Christian knights, Saracen champions, virtuous and not so virtuous ladies, and a string of other characters, often with little or no connection to the main plot. The war thus provides a loose framework for the narrative, which is brought back to it from time to time only to depart again in another direction. Yet the war and Orlando's love and madness are closely allied: love makes him abandon his duty as Charlemagne's champion in pursuit of the beautiful Angelica, and when it becomes madness, seriously delays the ultimate Christian victory. Orlando is brought back to his wits and to his duty by the English knight Astolfo who, in an episode that encapsulates much of Ariosto's distinctive wit, is sent by St John to the moon to collect Orlando's senses, and his own, from a valley full of all sorts of lost objects, of which the section containing people's lost senses is by far the largest. It is not just Orlando, but most, if not all, of the characters who have lost their senses in one way or another, just as, says the author, he has also lost them himself.

The centrifugal tendency of the narrative comes in part from the characters' tendency to follow where their impulses lead them, typically in pursuit of love, and largely unconstrained by the demands of both ordinary life and Christian duty. While he usually condemns breaches of the code of chivalry such as cowardice or avarice, Ariosto generally looks on moral weakness with amused tolerance. When Ruggiero comes across the naked Angelica chained to a rock, his immediate impulse is to take advantage of the situation to rape her, and Ariosto, in one of many ostensibly authorial comments, suggests that it would be unrealistic to expect anything else. However, as Ruggiero struggles to take off his armour in order to have his way, Angelica eludes him by making herself invisible. The episode is emblematic: characters seem free in the *Furioso* to pursue their desires without criticism, but they generally fail to attain them. If Orlando neglects his duty by abandoning Charlemagne to pursue Angelica, he is only doing the same as everyone else in the poem. And he too fails: he goes mad because Angelica, the daughter of the Emperor of Cathay and the most beautiful woman in the world, falls in love with Medoro, a simple foot-soldier. She tends his wounds and escapes with him back to China.

Desire is also essentially illusory. Angelica is not what Orlando thinks she is or what he wants her to be. As Ariosto says of one of her Saracen suitors, love makes one see the invisible, and makes invisible what one sees. The idea recurs insistently with the magician Atlante, who repeatedly tries to forestall the predicted early death of Ruggiero, once his ward, and creates a magic castle in which he traps the characters by whom Ruggiero might be killed, and where they run from room to room oblivious of each other, all in pursuit of an illusory image of the object or person they most desire. The men may be ideals of prowess and bravery,

12. Giovanni Battista Tiepolo, *Angelica Coming to the Aid of the Wounded Medoro* (fresco, 1757) from the Room of Orlando Furioso in the Villa Valmarana ai Nani, Vicenza. The subject retained its attraction over two centuries after the poem was written

the women of beauty, but their powers of understanding are irredeemably impaired. Chance and coincidence also play a major part: Christian knights, Saracens, and ladies travel from country to country, but accidental encounters or events constantly cause their journeys to change direction. Towards the end of the poem, Ruggiero sails to Africa and in mid-journey a violent storm arises that causes crew and passengers to abandon ship. All drown except Ruggiero, yet once the ship has been abandoned, the storm subsides and, without a crew, the ship sails straight to its destination. Humans are the playthings of forces beyond human understanding, with no discernible design: if destiny or fate have a role, it is only in a selective and arbitrary fashion, since it is the random whims of fortune which rule our lives. Nearly four centuries separate Ariosto and Svevo, but intellectually they are close.

For much of those intervening centuries radical secularism was largely suppressed, when it existed at all. The Counter-Reformation, the Catholic Church's response to the Protestant Reformation initiated by Luther, gave the literature of the later 16th century a strongly pious and observant content. Tasso's *Gerusalemme liberata* is about the triumph of religion in a way that Ariosto's epic certainly is not, though the tensions in Tasso's poem show how hard it was to integrate the demands of imagination and emotion with religious orthodoxy. Tensions and fractures will haunt the literature that follows. At one extreme is a mass of pious hagiography and sermonizing; at the other, a work such as Marino's *Adone* (1623), the most celebrated literary product of the Italian baroque, which uses the story of Venus and Adonis for an exuberant and shameless celebration of the delights of the senses and of its own artifice. But conformism had the upper hand. Seventeenth-century 'libertine' writers, who challenged the power of the Church in the name of freedom of thought, frequently paid for their temerity with their lives; in any case, they were little read, if they were published at all. Yet literary and scientific academies kept the intellectual traditions alive, and in Naples Giambattista

Vico formulated a novel, quite un-Christian, vision of the nature and history of human society, though it was only in the 20th century that his major work, the *Scienza nova* (*New Science*, 1744), was given due recognition. Things did begin to change in the mid-18th century as the French Enlightenment was taken up in the more progressive Italian states, and Italian Enlightenment thinkers (*illuministi*) attempted to bring themselves and their country up to date with the scientific and social thought of the rest of Europe. It was from the confluence of Enlightenment ideas and the native humanist tradition that the secularism of Foscolo and Leopardi emerged and assumed the distinctive shape that it would maintain into the 20th century.

It is not surprising that secularism remains a dominant trend in 20th-century literature from Svevo and Pirandello onwards; more striking is writers' continued pessimism. We have already discussed Pavese's conviction of the essential impossibility of human fulfilment; other writers direct their attention more at the distinctive problems of the modern world, expressing a deeply negative view of life in the 20th century, though usually with the conviction that literature can help in its own way to deal with it. One of the severest commentators on modernity was Alberto Moravia, another of the thoroughly secularized Jewish writers of his generation along with Bassani, Natalia Ginzburg, and Primo Levi. Moravia's first novel, *Gli indifferenti* (translated as *The Time of Indifference*), was published in 1929 when he was only twenty-two, and drew an uncompromising picture of the moral indifference and lassitude of contemporary middle-class youth. The novel has been read as anti-Fascist, and Moravia did go on to write some fairly heavy-handed committed fiction as well as celebrations of lower-class vitality, most notoriously *La romana* (*The Woman of Rome*) which recounts the career of a Roman prostitute. But his main subject was always middle-class 'corruption', as he saw it. In the 'essay-novels' of the 1960s and later, the analysis became ruthlessly explicit, exposing the alienation of middle-class families from reality through their fetishism of sex and money, particularly the former. A mother tries to prostitute her daughter in *L'attenzione (Paying Attention)*, another mother allows her young son to watch her having sex with her lover in *Il viaggio a Roma (Journey to Rome)*, a father seduces his daughter-in-law in *L'uomo che guarda (The Watching Man)*, a man has all his actions dictated to him (literally) by his penis in *Io e lui (Me and Him)*. Narratives such as these may be comic, shocking, or disgusting, and seemed quite risqué when they were first published, but there is nothing particularly pornographic about them. The sexual encounters are invariably failures, instances of people's inability to have real human relationships with one another. Moravia described himself as a humanist, but it is humanism of an extraordinarily negative kind. Despair, he wrote, was the natural condition of man in the modern world, and the task of the writer is simply to face up to it by making modern alienation the subject of his work. The only solution seems to be the sort of disengagement represented in *La noia (Boredom)* and *L'attenzione*, whose narrators eventually attain a state of benign and detached contemplation of the human situations they were otherwise unable to deal with.

In this one respect, the later Moravia is similar to Calvino, in feeling that literary commitment in the modern world is achieved through representing its general problems, not through espousing a party or an ideology. Other writers, reeling from the traumas of Fascism and the war, and appalled by government failures and the economic and social transformations of the 1950s and 1960s, were much more bleak. We have already noted the political pessimism of Sciascia. Bassani's only novel about the post-war world, and probably his most pessimistic, *L'airone (The Heron, 1968)*, recounts the last day in the life of a Ferrarese landowner, who commits suicide as a result of his disgust with the world in which he lives. All in all, it is rare to find a novel of any stature from the 20th century that ends in contentment or reconciliation, though the case of Primo Levi stands out as an unexpected exception. His *Se questo è un uomo (If This Be a Man, 1947)*, an autobiographical account of survival in the Auschwitz death-camp, deals with its dreadful subject in a resolutely secular spirit, and with an extraordinary analytical and ironic intelligence. A later, fictional work, *La chiave a stella* (*The Wrench*, 1978), provides a kind of positive complement to this subject, developing a latter-day humanist ethic based on the celebration of work as the application of intelligence to the solution of concrete problems. Even here, however, one might find traces of the despair which seems eventually to have driven Levi to suicide in 1987.

* * *

Secular humanism, especially in its more pessimistic forms, is one of the reasons why the Italian literary canon has always seemed remote from the Catholic majority. For them, there was of course always another literature, written as well as oral, which did cater for and conform with various forms of popular beliefs and attitudes – stories, sermons, lives of saints, narrative poems by professional improvisers (*cantastorie*) about Orlando and other heroes, and so on. A good deal of this was in dialect. In the 13th and 14th centuries, for instance, there was a tradition of *laude*, religious praise-songs that were publicly performed and sung, reaching a high point with the Franciscan friar Jacopone da Todi. Dialect writing, in his case Umbrian, was by no means necessarily conformist. Jacopone was as vehement in his poems denouncing Pope Boniface VIII as Dante ever was in the *Divine Comedy*, and was imprisoned for his pains until he publicly recanted. Later dialect poets could be equally subversive. The 18th-century Venetian Giorgio Baffo was a polemical cultivator of libertine obscenity. In the next century, Giuseppe Gioachino Belli's more than two thousand sonnets in Roman dialect present popular life in pre-Unification Rome with disillusioned scepticism about religious practices and beliefs in the very heart of Christendom. But a perceived need for a valid Christian literature certainly remained and was forcefully voiced by the Milanese Romantics of the post-Napoleonic years. It was partly in the light of their aspirations that Manzoni, not long a convert to Catholicism as well as to the idea of the novel, embarked on the *Promessi sposi*.

We have already indicated that Manzoni's religion is not straightforward. Conventional though some of the novel's moralizing may be, it also raises disquieting issues in Christian thought, not least through his tendency to give more importance to the interventions of Divine Grace than to the sinner's willingness to repent. The tension with orthodox belief returns in a different form in Manzoni's most prominent successor as a Catholic writer, Antonio Fogazzaro, whose novels express the conflicting aspirations and ideas of his main readers, the northern middle classes of the post-Unification decades. *Piccolo mondo antico* (*Little World of the Past*, 1895), a nostalgic recreation of love and life in the rural Valsolda in the years leading up to Unification, has humour, richness of colour and characterization, plus (unusually for Fogazzaro and the Italian novel as a whole) an engaging plot, and is one of the best Italian novels of its time. Italian nationalism, Christian faith and respect for the Church, the need for social order and horror at revolutionary socialism, dialect and the national language, marriage and adulterous desire, are all brought together in the interests of a higher harmony. But again there were problems: Fogazzaro made his harmony up to date by integrating into it a spiritualized version of Darwinian ideas on evolution, and thereby risked the ire of the Church. To his horror, his 1903 novel *Il santo* (*The Saint*) was put on the Index and his popularity went into decline. The problem of writing good literature which at the same time accords with Catholic beliefs is not just an Italian one. European literature from the Middle Ages onwards effectively asserts its independence from ecclesiastical authority. But the issue has been particularly keenly felt throughout the history of Italian literature, which has had to struggle repeatedly for that independence, however gloomy a form it might take, and has found the path of reconciliation with the Church particularly hard.

Chapter 6
Women

Un uomo in una donna, anzi uno dio per la sua bocca parla

[A man within a woman, no a god, speaks through her mouth]
(Michelangelo)

Dante's account of his final reunion with Beatrice is one of the most moving, dramatic, and rich moments in the *Divine Comedy*. It is also one of the most surprising. Dante has been persuaded to make his journey through Hell because Virgil, his guide, had received his instructions from Beatrice, and it is the thought of Beatrice that drives him on. Now at the top of Mount Purgatory, Dante emerges from a barrier of fire into the Earthly Paradise, the Garden of Eden where Adam and Eve were created. It takes time for Beatrice to appear; when she does, it is at the centre of a long and complex symbolic pageant that unfolds before Dante's eyes. The part before Beatrice represents the history of the human race up to the coming of Christ; but if Christ is present at all in the pageant, it is in allegorical form, as a gryphon drawing the chariot carrying Beatrice, who to all intents and purposes has taken his place. She will then have an active role in the part of the pageant still to come, which will continue the story into the present and future. That is in itself a startling promotion, not just for a figure who has her origin in a Florentine girl of no prominence outside Dante's work, but even for the most adored of courtly ladies in medieval literature, including the Beatrice of the *Vita nova*. From a few years after Dante's death, readers have wanted to allegorize her. If she really represents Theology or Divine Grace, then the problem of what she is doing in a procession representing the whole of human history can be made to disappear.

Allegory may indeed be intended; even so, Dante chooses to personalize and complicate the encounter. He represents himself as thrown into emotional chaos first by the sudden, distressing disappearance of Virgil, and then by Beatrice's attitude, which is anything but welcoming or approving. After all that he has been through for her sake, she exacts from him a painful, heartfelt confession of his errors, principally for forgetting her and going after other women, who themselves may or may not be allegorical figures. She behaves like an abandoned lover who will only forgive and forget at a price, he like a man who finds in the beloved an erotic fascination he has repressed or forgotten. Contrary to most allegorical practice, the emphasis falls throughout on the individuality of the three protagonists – Virgil, wept over rather than transcended; Dante, mentioned here by name for the only time in the whole poem; and Beatrice, who asserts her presence and her power with sarcastic vehemence. Beatrice will then become Dante's firm, loving, and knowledgeable guide through the heavens of Paradise, until St Bernard takes over for the final approach to the Godhead, and in this role she is easier to allegorize. But the encounter in the Earthly Paradise seems deliberately to bring together personal and universal experience, allegorical and literal representation, orthodox and unconventional ideas, and blend them in a unique synthesis, more poetic than intellectual – though Dante seems to insist that his readers should do their utmost to decipher the meaning or meanings of the encounter, and most commentators from the 14th century onwards have found themselves doing just that.

Dante's other female characters are inevitably seen in relation to Beatrice. Some embody her saintly or her allegorical aspects; the most famous of them, Francesca da Rimini, is a kind of anti-Beatrice, whose adulterous passion has meant her eternal damnation, but who has a direct human and poetic appeal. In the immediate aftermath of the *Divine Comedy*, Petrarch rethought Beatrice in his Laura, as we discussed in Chapter 2, and through him an idealized Beatrice-Laura would live on as the staple *donna* of Italian poetry. But Dante had not disposed of the adulterous female lover by putting her in Hell, his representation of Francesca being anyway too ambivalent for that. In the mid-14th century, she made a return or series of returns, which at least on the face of it seemed to sweep all Beatrices and Lauras aside.

Boccaccio's *Decameron*, completed in Florence in the early 1350s, is the culmination of a career as a story-teller, in verse and prose, that had begun in Naples, where he had been sent in his teens to work for a branch of the Florentine banking family, the Bardi. There, he had access to the court of the French ruler Robert of Anjou and to the French romances that were its favourite literary entertainment. His early works are largely retellings of French love stories in Italian, almost all in strikingly innovative ways. At least two were European successes: the *Filostrato* is taken up by Chaucer in *Troilus and Criseyde*, and through him by Shakespeare; the *Teseida*, a romance pretending to be a classical epic, becomes Chaucer's *Knight's Tale*. From the start, love in Boccaccio has a strong physical side with no aspirations to transcendence, and may or may not lead to marriage, though the earthliness does not mean a commitment to realism, each of Boccaccio's earlier works being primarily an experiment with existing literary conventions. The hundred *novelle* of the *Decameron* mark a major change. Out goes any overt classicism, though some more or less romance plots stay, and in comes the short story, or *novella*, with plots from story collections and other not particularly elevated sources, presumably including oral ones. The most striking innovation is that the stories are now firmly grounded in recognizable social realities; many characters have names of identifiable individuals, live in Florence and other cities or at the courts of historical rulers, and make and lose money by trading or banking or through sheer luck. Most are merchants and their wives and daughters, though there are also kings, nobles, workmen, peasants, nuns, friars, and priests. In this world, sexuality is paramount, sometimes satirically, often comically, and always with full recognition of its power across the genders and the classes, including the clergy, who are fiercely denounced for their hypocrisy at various points, but who almost always manage to satisfy their needs unscathed. Women are ready lovers, before, inside, and outside marriage. In the freest, comic stories, they become active and resourceful dupers of their husbands, not all of whom are old and impotent, though there are other stories, some of them tragic, in which the woman is a more thoughtful, dignified, and articulate lover. It is easy to feel that the sin of Dante's Francesca has been turned upside down, when we read the story of Nastagio degli Onesti (5.8), the plot of which turns on the vision of a young woman dreadfully punished in the afterlife for having driven her lover to his death through her coldness. Not only does the vision make the woman Nastagio loves change her attitude; it apparently makes all the girls of Ravenna, where the story is set, more receptive to love.

Yet Boccaccio is not preaching sexual freedom for women, or for men either, even if individual stories might seem quite anarchic. There are well-established conventions about love at work here – for instance, that young women and old husbands do not go together, or that the true lover has in some way a right to expect his beloved to return his love. In any case, literary filters hold the material at a distance. The stories are told over ten days by ten young people, seven women and three men, from the merchant aristocracy of Florence, in the gardens of an exquisite villa just outside the city to which they move to escape the plague of 1348. Of the narrators, in contrast to the figures in the stories, we know the pseudonyms and precious little else, and their generally brief comments on the stories tell us little about their stance on the moral and sexual issues raised. Neither do Boccaccio's ambiguous interventions in his own person. The very last story chronicles the virtues of Griselda, the poor girl abruptly taken in marriage by a noble husband, who puts up uncomplainingly with a prolonged series of gratuitous and increasingly monstrous cruelties from him, and then happily accepts restoration to wifely dignity when he finally offers it. Petrarch wrote in his last letter to Boccaccio that this was the only serious story in a frivolous youthful work, and translated it into Latin, taking out some of the innuendos at the beginning and end which suggest that Boccaccio was not quite so serious as Petrarch wanted him to be. It was his translation which made Patient Griselda a European figure, who could be allegorized as a representation of the soul's proper relationship to the tests God inflicts on humanity. That was certainly far from Boccaccio. He did move back to more obviously orthodox attitudes after the *Decameron*: his next and last imaginative work in Italian, the *Corbaccio* (*Crow*), was a misogynistic denunciation of women of almost comic ferocity. Yet his position remained ambiguous. The *De mulieribus claris* (*On Famous Women*) is an erudite encyclopaedia in Latin charting the virtues (mostly) of a hundred women of antiquity, with six moderns tacked on at the end. The readership was presumably in the first instance mostly male. In his late vernacular biography of Dante, on the other hand, he expresses approval of Dante's decision to write in the vernacular and hence create a work that could be read by women and other uneducated people, while at the same time criticizing him for getting married.

The ambiguities in the great authors of the 14th century continue to resurface in Italian literature, even as late as the 19th and 20th centuries. Patient Griselda is reincarnated in Lucia, the heroine of Manzoni's *Promessi sposi*, the fallen woman in his anti-heroine, the Nun of Monza. In a more rationalist spirit, a Platonic Beatrice figure returns with Leopardi's vision of the idealized non-existent lady in his poem 'Alla sua donna' ('To His Lady'). Montale builds his most powerful poetry around a semi-mythic figure whom he explicitly casts as a re-working of Beatrice and Laura, one that provides him (and by extension his readers) with a core of positive values to set against the barbarity of Fascism and the war into which it led the country. Micòl in the *Giardino dei Finzi-Contini* may be the incarnation of 1930s chic and sharpness, but she is also Bassani's version of a lost, unknowable Laura. Conversely, the assertive earthbound woman of Boccaccio is already relegated to the comic margins in the Renaissance, and makes only muted reappearances thereafter. Goldoni, for instance, includes some vigorous lower-class women in some comedies (notably Mirandolina in *La locandiera*), but neutralizes any threat to the social order with his endings. Only in the late 19th century will D'Annunzio, and other writers who take up contemporary Pan-European decadence, produce a new form of female heroine – mysterious, wayward, beautiful, demanding, and arid, though also largely literary in origin. The threat to the male order is evident. In the next century, it would be given its most sceptical and entertaining articulation by Vitaliano Brancati, whose *Don Giovanni in Sicilia* (1941) and *Il bell'Antonio* (*Handsome Antonio*, 1949) play on the clash between the male protagonists' need to flaunt their sexual potency and their actual inadequacy as lovers. In not quite such flamboyant terms, the issue of male sexual failure would haunt much other fiction of the mid-20th century.

* * *

This curious regressiveness is by no means the whole story. From the early 15th century, if not earlier, literate women began to increase in number and to write and publish in their own names. While the humanists would by and large stay with Latin and away from contemporary women and the whole thematics of love literature, there was a current which envisaged extending serious education to girls. One or two women in the 15th century had the Latin and the strength of character to put forward forceful feminist arguments themselves, even if, as happened with the young Brescian writer Laura Cereta, they were strongly criticized for doing so and, what was worse, doing so in public. By the next century, the case for considering women as having more potential than had been traditionally allowed was being debated more seriously in the vernacular, though even the strongest advocates show a certain unease. Castiglione's *Cortegiano* constructs a female courtier, a *donna di corte* who is, at least up to a point, educated, intelligent, and articulate, as well as beautiful and virtuous. But this figure is defined by male participants, one of whom has grave doubts about the whole idea, and of the two women present, one, the Duchess who presides over the discussions, remains almost entirely silent, and the other, Emilia Pia, is restricted to punctuating the speeches of the men with brief, sharp-witted comments.

Literacy among women of the upper classes was spreading, however, and print had made vernacular literary models, Petrarch in particular, and the freshly formalized Italian language widely available. Women now began to write and publish Petrarchist lyric poetry in their own persons. There had been one shadowy woman poet in 13th-century Florence, whom we know as La Compiuta Donzella, that is, the 'Accomplished Maid', though Compiuta may have been her given name. Two of her three surviving sonnets stand out thematically against the male poetry of the time: one complains about being forced by her father to marry a man she does not love, and in the second she says that she intends to get away from the horror of men by entering a nunnery. After that, women's poetry is hard to find until a sudden and highly successful profusion in the 16th century. Vittoria Colonna's *Rime* of 1539 was one of the most printed collections of the century, and the 1559 anthology of *Rime diverse d'alcune nobilissime e virtuosissime donne* (*Various Rhymes of Certain Most Noble and*

Virtuous Ladies) includes 52 names. It was, of course, compiled and edited by a man, Ludovico Domenichi.

Women's poetry includes what we are likely to see as some of the most interesting and individual variations on the literary conventions of the time, in part because a woman could not simply appropriate the male versions. A woman could not praise the beauty and virtues of her beloved or express desire in the same way, without breaching the confines of decorum. Italian criticism (by men) has often talked condescendingly of the simplicity and directness of the best poetry by women. In reality, the approach to writing was as self-conscious as that of male writers, any apparent modesty being a way of finding a voice that was socially acceptable. This was true even in the morally relaxed society of Venice in the mid-16th century. Gaspara Stampa, who moved there from Padua, writes primarily about her eventually unhappy love for a man of more noble rank than herself, emphasizing her own insignificance as a person and her incapacities as a poet. But there was still a problem of exposure. Even though her collected poems were not published until after her death, Stampa had to deal with accusations of whorishness, and the suspicions have still not been entirely dispelled. At least one notable woman took the opposite tack and pushed more firmly against the limits of respectability: Veronica Franco was a high-class professional courtesan in Venice and produced a more relaxed and self-confident poetry, generally in *terza rima* sequences (*capitoli*) rather than sonnets, in which a still decorous Petrarchist idiom allows acknowledgement of sensual desire and its pleasures. It probably could not last. Under pressure from the Inquisition, Franco's career ended in repentance. As the Counter-Reformation gathered force, all writers found themselves having to confront religious issues with a new seriousness. The seriousness is particularly evident in Vittoria Colonna, a member of one of the oldest Roman families and widow of the Marquis of Pescara. Her earlier poetry celebrates her husband, who died in 1525, and with whom she hopes to be reunited eventually in heaven. That in itself was laudable enough to bring her praise, but the redoubtable Colonna became more and more assertively spiritual, inside and outside her poetry, to the point of risking the ire of the Inquisition. Michelangelo paid her what he and his male contemporaries no doubt considered one of the highest possible compliments in the

13. Michelangelo, drawing of Vittoria Colonna. The idealized, almost masculine figure corresponds to the image of her suggested by his poetry

lines at the head of this chapter, by saying that she spoke like a
man or a god in a woman's body.

Other women writing towards the end of the century and in the
first decades of the next wrote polemical treatises and dialogues
which have only recently been given the attention they deserved.
Modesta Pozzo de' Zorzi, another 16th-century Venetian who wrote
as Moderata Fonte, had composed poetry as a young woman but
effectively stopped on marriage. She later returned to writing with a
remarkable dialogue in two books, *Il merito delle donne* (*The Merit
of Ladies*), which was published in 1600, eight years after her death.
The setting is a delightful garden in the Venetian house of the
young widow Leonora, where she and six other women of various
ages meet and talk about the problem of men under the benign
queenship of Corinna, the oldest woman in the group. The echoes
of Boccaccio, Castiglione, and many Renaissance dialogues are
evident, but so too are the novelties. The first day becomes mostly
criticism, at times denunciation, of male behaviour and attitudes,
embracing husbands, lovers, fathers, and sons. Against the violence
and hypocrisy of men are set the intelligence, reliability, generosity,
and general moral decency of women. But, true to the moderation
suggested by her pseudonym, Moderata Fonte keeps a certain
lightness and variety of tone, as if her speakers are actually running
through a string of well-known points, which for the most part they
are. On the second day, Corinna gives the others a string of lessons
on everything from astronomy and geography to birds, plants,
medicine, and literature. It is all serious and light-hearted at the
same time, and a long way from the rather ponderous and didactic
tone of many Renaissance dialogues by men, whilst demonstrating
that women can appropriate male forms of discourse and
knowledge and give them a distinctive twist. After a lengthy,
seemingly felt, appeal to men to behave better, in the concluding
discussion a young unmarried girl, who has been convinced by
everything that has been said that she should not marry, is talked
back into the idea; there are after all exceptions to the rule that men
are insufferable. Determinedly cheerful though it is, the book

expects the reader to think about the issues and to make up her (or his) mind about how to deal with them.

Women writers who tackled these issues also included some who were more uncompromising and even less read, such as Arcangela Tarabotti, whose denunciations of male abuse begin with *L'inferno monacale* (*The Hell of the Nunnery*, c. 1640), an attack, grounded in her own painful experiences, on the practice of forcing unwanted daughters into convents. But scope for writing by women was already narrowing. Over the next two centuries, few figures emerge. Some noblewomen wrote verse or held literary salons in the 18th century; others became famous even outside Italy for their performances as poetic improvisers; a few were successful journalists. One of the most famous of these, Eleonora Fonseca Pimentel, became the public voice of the republic of Naples of 1799. When it fell, she was hanged with seven other leading Jacobins after Lord Nelson reneged on the protection he had promised.

* * *

The Risorgimento had various women heroes at its moments of drama. But it was only in the later 19th century, as literacy increased and with it the number of women readers, that there emerged a strong current of fiction by women, many of them also active as campaigning journalists. Though read with much greater gusto and much more widely than Manzoni and other prominent male authors, successful novelists such as Carolina Invernizio, with more than a hundred books to her credit, have been regularly dismissed for having produced *romanzi d'appendice* – the term comes from the serialization of novels in supplements to daily papers and indicates a melodramatic and formulaic sort of fiction. Others competed more directly for the high ground with their male contemporaries, sometimes with considerable public success. Grazia Deledda, for instance, was awarded the Nobel Prize in 1926, somewhat to the surprise of most Italians, for her dour representations of life in her native Sardinia. But there is no Italian Jane Austen, Emily Brontë, or Virginia Woolf, just as in poetry there is no Emily Dickinson or even Christina Rossetti. In part, the reasons lie in the still limited readership, and also in the tenacity of traditional mind-sets which women writers constantly had to confront. The autobiographical novel of the time that confronts the issues directly, and became something of a banner-work for later feminists, is *Una donna* (*A Woman*, 1906) by Sibilla Aleramo, the pseudonym of Rina Faccio, which recounts the struggle of a young woman to make an independent writing career for herself, at the cost in the end of abandoning her husband and son. That struggle led Aleramo and other women writers into enthusiastic support for Mussolini, and with some justification. Particularly in its earlier years, the Fascist revolution went against its own rhetoric and extended the possibilities open to women. One sign of this is that in the 1930s more fiction by women was published in Italy than ever before. From this perspective, the Resistance and its culture was more of a throwback. Even if some of the most telling accounts of the partisan struggles are by women, the return to a kind of normality after the war was for many women a return to traditional roles, even within the revolutionary Left. It would take several decades of social and economic upheaval and a crusading feminist movement to make serious and probably lasting changes.

One of the authors who best articulates crucial moments of change in Italian society from the 1940s through to the 1970s is Natalia Ginzburg, an avowed non-feminist who nonetheless looks at things from a perspective quite different from that of her male contemporaries. There is a particularly striking contrast with Pavese, her tormented sexist friend with whom she worked as a publishing editor for Einaudi in Turin in the immediate post-war years. Like many other modern novelists, male and female, Ginzburg looks more to other European writers than to the Italian tradition when creating a voice for herself. From Proust, she takes a fascination with the techniques of memory: her most popular book, *Lessico famigliare* (*Family Sayings*, 1963), is an affectionate memoir of growing up in a middle-class Jewish family in Turin in the 1930s, with Fascism gradually changing from something her father can dismiss as an absurd charade into a threat to their very existences. The book's force and often unexpected comedy come from relying on ostensibly insignificant details and quirks of behaviour to bring back a whole world of the past, much as Proust does. The manner, though, owes more to the eccentrically flat style of the English novelist Ivy Compton-Burnett, whose work Ginzburg got to know when her second husband went to work at the Italian Institute in London in 1947. The result in Italian is a stylization which many (male) critics deemed a non-style, especially in its earlier realizations, though it gradually became more relaxed, proving an ideal medium for distanced but sympathetic depictions of often deeply painful experiences.

Ginzburg's earlier and later novels have much of the deep pessimism about human relationships to be found in the writers we considered in the last chapter. But in her last two particularly, something more positive is added. *Caro Michele* (*Dear Michael*, 1973) and *La città e la casa* (*The City and the House*, 1984) are epistolary novels about relationships within a family and group of friends, which exploit the full potential of the genre to convey a fragmentary and contradictory view of these relationships; indeed the novels as a whole are fragmentary, with wandering and diffuse plots, unexpected tragic developments, and not much in the way of conclusions. This structure, or lack of it, is integrally connected to the view of relationships and life that the novels convey, as puzzling, incoherent, and directionless. The central figures of both, if there are any, are middle-aged parents, a woman in the first and a man in the second: no longer married, without careers, and with awkward, cautious, but affectionate feelings for their children – particularly awkward in the case of the sons in each book, both of whom represent a distinctly younger generation, and who both die sudden and violent deaths. However, the pessimism is far from unrelieved. There is interest and enjoyment in the details of domestic life, including possessions and houses; and more profoundly, there is a cool but serious appreciation of people's individuality, of the virtues of kindness and honesty, and above all of the benefits of memory. Despite all their failures and difficulties, the central characters have a firm sense of the pleasures and values of life, however occasional and elusive they may be.

It is arguable that over the last three decades a situation of gender parity has established itself in Italian literature in a way that may not be the case in the country as a whole. Some of the most significant poets to have emerged over the last twenty years or so have been women. Antonella Anedda, Patrizia Cavalli, Iolanda Insana, Amelia Rosselli, Patrizia Valduga, and others do not form a school (schools as such have vanished in Italy as they have elsewhere), but all tend to bring into contemporary poetry ideas associated particularly with feminist thinking, such as the experience of marginalization or the search for alternatives to patriarchal language and thought. Like some of their male contemporaries, they are working to find a purchase on states of mind that resonate with a wide range of readers of both sexes in the modern West. Contemporary women's fiction is even stronger. Rosetta Loy and Dacia Maraini explore in various ways the historical novel and fictionalized personal memoir; Paola Capriolo manufactures steely fairy stories for adults. Together, they are probably the most interesting and accomplished Italian novelists since Calvino.

Further reading

General reference

P. Brand and L. Pertile (eds.), *The Cambridge History of Italian Literature* (Cambridge University Press, 1996). Narrative history also covering opera, with ample bibliography.

L. Panizza and S. Wood (eds.), *A History of Women's Writing in Italy* (Cambridge University Press, 2000). Up-to-date narrative history.

P. Hainsworth and D. Robey (eds.), *The Oxford Companion to Italian Literature* (Oxford University Press, 2003). Comprehensive alphabetical reference work, covering authors, trends, and historical events.

Histories of Italy

C. Duggan, *A Concise History of Italy* (Cambridge University Press, 2001). Excellent introductory survey.

P. Ginsborg, *Italy and its Discontents: Family, Civil Society and State* (Allen Lane, 2001). Comprehensive analysis of contemporary Italy.

C. Duggan, *The Force of Destiny: A History of Italy since 1796* (Allen Lane, 2007). The most up-to-date general account in English.

The Italian language

B. Migliorini, *The Italian Language*, abridged and recast by T. G. Griffith (Faber, 1966). Historical account with emphasis on literary usage.

A. L. Lepschy and G. Lepschy, *The Italian Language Today* (Routledge, 1988). General examination of modern Italian, taking into account regional and social variations.

M. Maiden, *A Linguistic History of Italian* (Longman, 1995). Approachable academic linguistic history.

Medieval and Renaissance literature

General studies

G. Holmes, *The Florentine Enlightenment* (Weidenfeld and Nicolson, 1969). Study of Florentine humanism in its context.

C. Kleinhenz, *The Early Italian Sonnet* (Milella, 1986). Survey of 13th- and early 14th-century practice.

P. Burke, *The Italian Renaissance: Culture and Society in Italy* (Polity, 1987). Examines literature and the arts in their social context.

V. Cox, *The Renaissance Dialogue* (Cambridge University Press, 1992). General history of the literary form.

M. McLaughlin, *Literary Imitation in the Italian Renaissance* (Oxford University Press, 1995). Examination of this important feature of Renaissance writing.

V. Cox, *Women's Writing in Italy 1400–1650* (Johns Hopkins University Press, 2008). Detailed comprehensive history of the subject.

Dante

K. Foster, *The Two Dantes* (Darton, Longman and Todd, 1977). Discusses the tension between the secular and religious sides of Dante.

G. Holmes, *Dante* (Oxford University Press, 1980). Excellent short introduction to Dante's life and work.

Richard Lansing (ed.), *The Dante Encyclopedia* (Garland, 2000). Covers works, characters, and events.

R. Jacoff (ed.), *The Cambridge Companion to Dante* (Cambridge University Press, 2007). Collection of essays on core aspects of Dante's work.

Petrarch

N. Mann, *Petrarch* (Oxford University Press, 1984). Excellent short introduction to Petrarch's career and works.

P. Hainsworth, *Petrarch the Poet* (Routledge, 1988). Study of the Italian poems in their literary and biographical context.

V. Kirkham and A. Maggi (eds.), *Petrarch: A Critical Guide to the Complete Works* (University of Chicago Press, 2009). Essays on all Petrarch's works, both Latin and Italian.

Boccaccio

V. Branca, *Boccaccio: The Man and His Works*, tr. R. Monges and D. J. McAuliffe (Harvester, 1976). General survey by Italy's foremost modern Boccaccio scholar.

G. Olson, *Literature as Recreation in the Later Middle Ages* (Cornell University Press, 1982). General study centred on Boccaccio.

D. Wallace, *Giovanni Boccaccio, Decameron* (Cambridge University Press, 1991). Readable introduction.

Other Renaissance authors

C. P. Brand, *Tasso* (Cambridge University Press, 1965).

C. P. Brand, *Ariosto* (Edinburgh University Press, 1974).

J. R. Woodhouse, *Baldesar Castiglione* (Edinburgh University Press, 1978).

Q. Skinner, *Machiavelli* (Oxford University Press, 1981).

C. Ryan, *The Poetry of Michelangelo* (Athlone Press, 1998).

A. Brundin, *Vittoria Colonna and the Spiritual Poetics of the Italian Reformation* (Ashgate Publishing, 2008)

Literature since the Renaissance

General studies

R. S. C. Gordon, *An Introduction to Twentieth-Century Italian Literature* (Duckworth, 2005). Discusses the major authors and issues.

A. H. Caesar and M. Caesar, *Modern Italian Literature* (Polity, 2007). History of literature from 1690 onwards.

Particular aspects

Z. G. Baranski and L. Pertile (eds.), *The New Italian Novel* (Edinburgh University Press, 1993). Essays on fiction from the 1960s onwards.

Z. G. Baranski and R. West (eds.), *The Cambridge Companion to Modern Italian Culture* (Cambridge University Press, 2001). Essays on cinema, art, and literature.

J. Burns, *Fragments of impegno: Interpretations of Commitment in Contemporary Italian Narrative, 1980–2000* (Northern Universities Press, 2001). Considers the political dimension of Tabucchi and others.

G. Bonsaver, *Censorship and Literature in Fascist Italy* (University of Toronto Press, 2007). Important discussion of relations between writers and the Fascist state.

Studies of selected modern authors

A. Alexander, *Giovanni Verga* (Grant & Cutler, 1972). Biography.

G. Carsaniga, *Giacomo Leopardi* (Edinburgh University Press, 1977).

D. Thompson, *Cesare Pavese: A Study of the Major Novels and Poems* (Cambridge University Press, 1982).

J. Gatt-Rutter, *Italo Svevo: A Double Life* (Oxford University Press, 1988). Biography.

J. R. Woodhouse, *Gabriele D'Annunzio, Defiant Archangel* (Oxford University Press, 1998). Biography.

M. McLaughlin, *Italo Calvino* (Edinburgh University Press, 1998).

M. Caesar, *Umberto Eco* (Polity, 1999).

G. Bonsaver, *Elio Vittorini: The Writer and the Written* (Northern Universities Press, 2007).

R. S. C. Gordon, *The Cambridge Companion to Primo Levi* (Cambridge University Press, 2007).

The *Writers of Italy* series, published by Edinburgh University Press, covers most of the major authors. A more recent series is *Italian Perspectives* (now published by Maney).

The University College Dublin Foundation for Italian Studies has published several collections of essays on Dante and studies of various more recent authors.

Appendix: writers cited

Alberti, Leon Battista (1404–1472). Humanist and architect.

Aleramo, Sibilla (1876–1950). Feminist novelist.

Alfieri, Vittorio (1749–1803). Playwright and autobiographer.

Anedda, Antonella (1958–). Poet.

Ariosto, Ludovico (1474–1533). Epic poet and humanist.

Baffo, Giorgio (1694–1768). Venetian dialect poet.

Bassani, Giorgio (1916–2000). Ferrarese novelist.

Beccaria, Cesare (1738–1794). Milanese Enlightenment thinker.

Belli, Giuseppe Gioachino (1791–1863). Roman dialect poet.

Bembo, Pietro (1470–1547). Venetian literary and linguistic theorist
    and cleric.

Boccaccio, Giovanni (1313–1375). Poet, short-story writer, and humanist.

Boiardo, Matteo Maria (?1441–1494). Ferrarese epic poet.

Brancati, Vitaliano (1907–1954). Sicilian novelist.

Bruni, Leonardo (?1370–1444). Florentine humanist.

Calvino, Italo (1923–1985). Novelist.

Camilleri, Andrea (1925–). Sicilian detective novelist.

Capriolo, Paola (1962–). Novelist.

Carducci, Giosuè (1835–1907). Poet and scholar.

Castiglione, Baldesar (1478–1529). Humanist and courtier.

Cavalcanti, Guido (?1260–1300). Poet.

Cavalli, Patrizia (1949–). Poet.

Cecco Angiolieri (c. 1260–1311/13). Comic poet.

Celati, Gianni (1937–). Novelist and story-writer.

Cereta, Laura (1469–1499). Humanist.

Colonna, Vittoria (1492–1547). Poet.

Compiuta Donzella, La (13th century). Poet.

Croce, Benedetto (1866–1952). Philosopher and critic.

D'Annunzio, Gabriele (1863–1938). Poet and novelist.

Dante Alighieri (1265–1321). Poet.

Deledda, Grazia (1871–1936). Sardinian novelist.

Della Casa, Giovanni (1503–1556). Humanist, poet, and cleric.

De Sanctis, Francesco (1817–1883). Neapolitan literary critic and historian.

Di Breme, Ludovico (1780–1820). Romantic polemicist.

Domenichi, Lodovico (1515–1564). Editor and translator.

Eco, Umberto (1932–). Theorist, journalist, and novelist.

Fenoglio, Beppe (1922–1963). Piedmontese novelist.

Ficino, Marsilio (1433–1499). Tuscan Neoplatonic philosopher.

Fo, Dario (1926–). Playwright.

Fogazzaro, Antonio (1841–1911). Catholic novelist.

Fonseca Pimentel, Eleonora (1752–1799). Neapolitan poet and journalist.

Fonte, Moderata (1555–1592). Venetian poet and protofeminist.

Fortini, Franco (1917–1994). Poet and critic.

Foscolo, Ugo (1778–1827). Novelist, poet, and critic.

Franco, Veronica (1546–1591). Venetian poet and courtesan.

Frederick II (1194–1250). Emperor, patron of literature, and occasional
    poet.

Gadda, Carlo Emilio (1893–1973). Milanese novelist.

Giacomo da Lentini (early 13th century). Sicilian poet.

Giannone, Pietro (1676–1748). Neapolitan lawyer and historian.

Ginzburg, Natalia (1916–1991). Novelist.

Goldoni, Carlo (1707–1793). Venetian playwright.

Guarino da Verona (1374–1460). Humanist educator.

Guicciardini, Francesco (1483–1540). Florentine historian and political
    theorist.

Guinizzelli, Guido (13th century). Bolognese poet.

Insana, Jolanda (1937–). Poet.

Invernizio, Carolina (1851–1916). Novelist.

Jacopone da Todi (1236–1306). Franciscan poet.

Leopardi, Giacomo (1798–1837). Poet and thinker.

Levi, Carlo (1902–1975). Piedmontese autobiographical writer and novelist.

Levi, Primo (1919–1987). Piedmontese autobiographical writer and novelist.

Loy, Rosetta (1931–). Novelist.

Machiavelli, Niccolò (1469–1527). Florentine political thinker and historian.

Manzoni, Alessandro (1785–1873). Milanese poet, tragedian, and novelist.

Maraini, Dacia (1936–). Roman novelist.

Marino, Giovanbattista (1569–1625). Poet.

Medici, Lorenzo de' (1449–1492). Patron of the arts and poet.

Meneghello, Luigi (1922–2007). Autobiographical writer and essayist.

Metastasio, Pietro (1698–1782). Poet and tragedian.

Michelangelo Buonarroti (1475–1564). Painter, sculptor, architect, and poet.

Montale, Eugenio (1896–1981). Poet.

Moravia, Alberto (1907–1990). Roman novelist.

Nievo, Ippolito (1831–1861). Novelist.

Parini, Giuseppe (1729–1799). Milanese satirical and moral poet.

Pascoli, Giovanni (1855–1912). Poet.

Pasolini, Pier Paolo (1922–1975). Poet, novelist, journalist, and film-maker.

Pavese, Cesare (1908–1950). Piedmontese novelist.

Petrarch, Francesco (1304–1374). Humanist and Italian poet.

Piccolomini, Enea Silvio (Pius II) (1405–1464). Humanist and Pope.

Pirandello, Luigi (1867–1936). Sicilian playwright.

Poliziano, Angelo (1454–1494). Tuscan humanist and Italian poet.

Rosselli, Amelia (1930–1996). Poet.

Sanguineti, Edoardo (1930–2010). Critic and avant-garde poet.

Sannazaro, Iacopo (1458–1530). Poet and pastoral writer.

Sarpi, Paolo (1552–1623). Venetian historian.

Saviano, Roberto (1979–). Journalist.

Sciascia, Leonardo (1921–1989). Sicilian novelist.

Sereni, Vittorio (1913–1983). Poet.

Silone, Ignazio (1900–1978). Novelist.

Stampa, Gaspara (1523–1554). Venetian poet.

Svevo, Italo (1861–1928). Triestine novelist.

Tabucchi, Antonio (1943–). Novelist.

Tarabotti, Arcangela (1604–1652). Venetian protofeminist.

Tasso, Torquato (1544–1595). Ferrarese epic and lyric poet.

Ungaretti, Giuseppe (1888–1970). Poet.

Valduga, Patrizia (1952–). Poet.

Verga, Giovanni (1840–1922). Sicilian novelist.

Vergerio, Pierpaolo (1370–1444). Humanist.

Vico, Giambattista (1668–1744). Neapolitan philosopher.

Vittorini, Elio (1908–1966). Novelist and theorist of culture.

Zanzotto, Andrea (1921–2011). Veneto poet.

Index

A

Academies 47, 48, 94
A ciascuno il suo 78
Adone 33, 94
Africa 28
Airone, L' 96
Alberti, Leon Battista 88, 117
Aleramo, Sibilla 110, 117
Alfieri, Vittorio 71, 117
alienation 96
Alighieri, Dante, *see* Dante
   Alighieri
allegory 27, 28, 47, 60, 63, 89,
   99–100, 103
Allegria, L' 25, 36
America 1, 13, 37, 64
Anedda, Antonella 112, 117
Angelica 92–3
anticlericalism 80, 86, 87
anti-Fascism 15–16, 37, 60, 76,
   79, 96
anti-Semitism 7
Arcadia (Academy) 33, 48
Arcadia (book) 33, 48
Ariosto, Ludovico 9, 32, 71, 89,
   90–4, 115, 117
aristocracy 49, 74, 102
Aristotle 64, 86
Armida 45, 46

Arnaut Daniel 29
Arthurian literature 91
asprezza 45
'A Silvia' 51
Astolfo 92
atheism 86
Atlante 93
Attenzione, L' 96
Augustine, St 29
Auschwitz 6, 96
Austen, Jane 109
Australia 1
Austria 1, 11, 33, 72, 73
autobiography 64
avant-garde, *see* neo-avant-garde
Avignon 28, 69

B

Baffo, Giorgio 97, 117
banking 9, 101, 102
Bardi family 101
Barone rampante, Il 77
baroque 32, 42
Bassani, Giorgio 5–9, 10, 18–19,
   20, 95, 96, 104, 117
Beatrice 27, 28, 29, 36, 65–9,
   99–101, 104
Beccaria, Cesare 71, 117
Bell'Antonio, Il 104

Belli, Giuseppe Gioachino 97, 117
Beltà, La 37
Bembo, Pietro 30, 31, 35, 40–1, 90, 117
Berlusconi, Silvio 19, 79
Bernard, St 100
Bettina 36
Bible 27
biography 28, 103
Boccaccio, Giovanni 2, 11, 14, 31, 32, 40–1, 43, 48, 88, 101–4, 115, 117
Boiardo, Matteo Maria 9, 10, 90–1, 117
Bologna 8, 18
Boniface VIII 97
Brancati, Vitaliano 104, 117
Brontë, Emily 109
Bruni, Leonardo 88, 117
Bufera e altro, La 39

C

Calvino, Italo 14, 55, 77–8, 79, 96, 112, 116, 117
Camilleri, Andrea 43, 117
camorra 79
Can Grande della Scala 47
canon 1–3
cantastorie 97
canzone 30, 51, 64
Canzoniere, Il 28–31, 69
Cavalieri, Tommaso 36
capitalism 6, 77
capitoli 106
Capriolo, Paola 112, 117
Carducci, Giosuè 5, 6, 24, 38, 117
Caro Michele 111
Carrara family 69
Castiglione, Baldesar 71, 91–3, 105, 115, 117
Catholics and Catholic church 16, 18, 20, 36, 70, 72, 79–80, 86, 89, 94, 97–8; *see also* Papacy
Cavaliere inesistente, Il 77

Cavalcanti, Guido 27, 117
Cavalli, Patrizia 112, 117
Cecco Angiolieri 35, 117
Celati, Gianni 43, 117
Cereta, Laura 105, 118
Charlemagne 77, 90, 91, 92
Chaucer, Geoffrey 101
Chiave a stella, La 97
chivalry 92
Christian religion 45, 72–5, 85–8, 92, 95, 98; *see also* Catholics and Catholic church
Christian Democrats 18–19
Cicero 88, 89
Città e la casa, La 111
classics and classicism 2, 29, 33, 36, 41, 45, 47, 50, 51, 64, 71, 72, 88, 101
Clorinda 45
Cola di Rienzo 69
Colonna, Vittoria 105, 107, 115, 118
Comedy 49, 86
Commedia, see *Divine Comedy*
commedia dell'arte 49
commentaries 35
communes 8, 67, 80
communists 6, 16, 17, 18, 57, 60, 64, 75, 77, 79
Compiuta Donzella, La 105, 118
Compton-Burnett, Ivy 111
Concordat 16
consumerism 77
Confessioni di un italiano, Le 73
Contesto, Il 78
Conversazione in Sicilia 62–3, 64, 75
Convivio, Il 27, 86
Corbaccio, Il 103
Corriere della sera, Il 14
Cortegiano, Il 89, 105
Coscienza di Zeno, La 12, 42, 81–3
Counter-Reformation 94, 106
courtesans 106
courts 9, 13, 15, 41, 90, 102, 106

Cristo si è fermato a Eboli 76
critics and criticism 24, 25, 32, 34, 36, 37, 47, 51, 55, 85, 106, 111
Croce, Benedetto 52, 118
Crusca, Accademia della 31, 41, 47

D

D'Annunzio, Gabriele 5, 24, 38, 104, 116, 118
Dante Alighieri 1, 2, 11, 14, 15, 26–7, 29, 30, 32, 34–6, 39, 41, 47–8, 59, 64–9, 73, 79, 86–8, 97, 99–101, 103, 114, 118
Darwin, Charles 51, 84, 85, 98
De Amore 88
decadence 104
Decameron 31, 41, 87, 101–3
decorum 35, 106
Dei sepolcri 86
Deledda, Grazia 109, 118
Della Casa, Giovanni 36, 118
democracy 6, 15
De mulieribus claris 103
De Sanctis, Francesco 2, 118
De Sica, Vittorio 55
detective fiction 79
De vulgari eloquentia 27
dialect(s) 2, 12, 15, 40, 42, 49, 74, 97–8
dialogues 28, 51, 89, 108, 114
Diario in pubblico 64
Di Breme, Ludovico 33, 118
Dickinson, Emily 110
dictionaries 31
Discorsi del poema eroico 44–5
Discorsi dell'arte poetica 44
Discorsi, I 70–1
Divine Comedy 1, 27, 29, 35, 47, 64–9, 89, 97, 99–101
dolce stil novo 27, 29
Domenichi, Lodovico 106, 118
Don Giovanni in Sicilia 104
Duce, Il, *see* Mussolini, Benito

E

Eco, Umberto 57–8, 116, 118
Economic miracle 6, 19
education 25, 87–8, 105
Einaudi 14, 110
emigration 1
engagement, *see impegno*
England and English 13, 34, 39, 64, 70, 76, 78
Enlightenment 41, 72, 95, 117
Enrico IV 53
epic 10, 28, 32, 44–5, 91, 94, 101
Erminia 45
essay-novel 55, 95
Este family 5–7, 9, 10, 92

F

fable 76
Farinata degli Uberti 87
Fascism 15–18, 37, 39, 40, 60, 76, 96, 111, 116
feminism 110, 112, 117
Fenoglio, Beppe 78, 118
Ferrara 5–10, 14, 24, 44, 90
Ficino, Marsilio 47, 90, 118
film 55
Filostrato, Il 101
Florence and Florentine 1, 9, 10, 12, 14, 15, 31, 35, 36, 41–2, 47, 60, 69, 70, 74, 89, 99, 101, 102, 105, 114
Fo, Dario 79, 118
Fogazzaro, Antonio 98, 118
Fonseca Pimentel, Eleonora 109, 118
Fontamara 12, 76
Fonte, Moderata 108, 118
Fortini, Franco 39, 118
fortuna 71, 74, 94
Foscolo, Ugo 38, 71, 86, 95, 118
France 1, 12, 13, 16, 39, 66, 74, 101
Francesca da Rimini 87, 101, 102
Franciscans 59, 97

Index

Franco, Veronica 106, 118
Frederick II 14, 118
French literature and culture 11,
    12, 26, 27, 39, 41, 64–5, 73, 74,
    95, 101
Freud, Sigmund 84–5
Futurism 25, 37, 49

G

Gadda, Carlo Emilio 42, 43, 118
Garibaldi, Giuseppe 11, 73
Genoa 9, 10
Germany 37, 81
Gerusalemme conquistata 44–6
Gerusalemme liberata 44–7, 94
Ghibellines, *see* Guelphs and
    Ghibellines
Giacomo da Lentini 30, 118
giallo, see detective fiction
Giannone, Pietro 71, 118
Giardino dei Finzi-Contini, Il 5–7,
    19, 24, 104
Giorno, Il 71
Giorno della civetta, Il 78
'Ginestra, La' 52
Ginzburg, Natalia 14, 95,
    110–11, 118
Giubbe Rosse 14
Goethe, Wolfgang von 71
Goldoni, Carlo 48–9, 118
Gomorra 79
Gracchi 60, 63
Greece and Greek 9, 34, 88
Griselda 103
Gruppo 63 79
Guarino da Verona 9, 118
Guelphs and Ghibellines 9, 15
Guicciardini, Francesco 70, 71, 118
Guinizzelli, Guido 118

H

hagiography 94
Hemingway, Ernest 64

Henry VII of Luxemburg 68
hermeticism (*ermetismo*) 25, 37
Hitler, Adolf 16
Horace 28, 29
humanism 9, 69, 88–90, 91, 94,
    97, 98

I

Idilli (Leopardi) 34, 51–2
Il fu Mattia Pascal 52
Illuminismo, see Enlightenment
impegno 20, 37, 39, 76–8, 116
improvisation 109
Indifferenti, Gli 95
industrialization 64, 77
Inferno 65–6, 68, 87
Inferno monacale, L' 109
Inquisition 107
Insana, Jolanda 112, 118
intellectuals 14, 18, 19, 20, 52, 55,
    78, 80
Invernizio, Carolina 109, 118
Io e lui 96
Italian (language) 1, 2, 11–12, 30,
    40–1, 74, 114

J

Jacobins 109
Jacopone da Todi 97, 118
Jews and Judaism 6–7, 18, 81, 85,
    95, 110
Joyce, James 81

K

Kafka, Franz 85

L

Langhe, Le 55, 56
language 1, 31, 32, 33, 40–3
Latin 2, 28, 30, 31, 47, 48, 69,
    103, 104

Latini, Brunetto 87
laude 97
Laura 28–9, 101, 104
Leopardi, Giacomo 2, 26, 33–4, 38, 50–2, 56, 86, 95, 104, 116, 118
Lessico Famigliare 110–1
letterati 20, 47
Levi, Carlo 76, 119
Levi, Primo, 95, 97, 116, 119
liberalism 72
libertinism 94, 97
literacy 15, 31, 40, 104, 105, 109
Livy 70
Locandiera, La 49, 104
Lombardy 41, 73
Loy, Rosetta 112, 119
Lucia 73, 103
Luna e i falò, La 55–7
Luther, Martin 94
lyric(ism) 27, 28, 29, 32, 36, 40, 51, 61, 62, 63, 86, 105

M

Machiavelli, Niccolò 70–1, 89, 115, 119
Mafia 78
maggiori, I 2
Malavoglia, I 74
Mallarmé, Stéphane 26
Mantua 10
Manzoni, Alessandro 2, 12, 38, 40–2, 72–3, 86, 97, 103, 109, 119
Maraini, Dacia 112, 119
Marche 33
Marco Lombardo 66
Marino, Giovanbattista 32, 94, 119
Mastro-don Gesualdo 75
'Mattina' 22–6, 36
Mazzini, Giuseppe 12
Medici, Giuliano de' 89
Medici, Lorenzo de' 14, 47, 89, 119
Medoro 93
Meneghello, Luigi 78, 119
merchants 14, 30, 102

Merito delle donne, Il 108
Mestiere di vivere, Il 55
Metastasio, Pietro, 119
metre 25, 36, 48
Michelangelo Buonarroti 36, 99, 107, 115, 119
Micòl 7, 104
Middle Ages 2, 8–9, 13, 14, 30, 59, 80, 98, 115
migration 19
Milan 9, 10, 14–15, 33, 41–2, 60, 62, 69, 72, 73, 97
Mirandolina 104
Modernism 17, 26, 37, 39, 61
Monarchia 66, 86
monarchism 69
Montale, Eugenio 2, 14, 16, 37–9, 81, 104, 119
Moravia, Alberto 55, 61, 95–6, 119
Moro, Aldo 18
Mussolini, Benito 15–17, 60, 62, 63, 110

N

Naples 10, 14, 71, 80, 94, 101, 109
Napoleon 10, 33, 71, 72, 86
Nastagio degli Onesti 102
nationalism 21, 46, 98
naturalism 15, 74
Nazis 15, 17, 63
Nelson, Lord 109
neo-avant-garde (*Neoavanguardia*) 37, 49, 58, 79
Neoplatonism 31, 89
Neorealism 42, 55
Nievo, Ippolito 73, 86, 119
nobility 10, 71, 75, 105
Noia, La 96
Nome della Rosa, Il 57–9
Normans 10
Northern League 19
Nostri antenati, I 77–8
novella 43, 101–2
Nun of Monza 104

O

obscenity 49, 97
Olindo 45
Opera aperta 58, 59
Operette morali 51
Orlando furioso 32, 90–3
Orlando innamorato 10, 90
Ossi di seppia 37, 39
otium 69
Ovid 29
Owen, Wilfred 22

P

Padua 106
Papacy 10, 11, 16, 59, 66–7, 69, 80,
    86–7
Paradiso 67–9, 100
Parini, Giuseppe 71, 119
Parma 10
Partigiano Johnny, Il 78
partisans 18, 57, 63, 77, 78, 110
Pascoli, Giovanni 25, 38, 119
Pasolini, Pier Paolo 39, 42, 43, 119
pastoral 28, 33, 48, 89
patronage 15
Pavese, Cesare 14, 55–8, 110,
    116, 119
peasants 14, 15, 41, 75, 76, 102
Pendolo di Foucault, Il 58
pessimism 33, 51, 80, 83, 85, 86,
    95, 97, 111
Petrarch, Francesco 2, 12, 14, 15,
    20, 26, 27–36, 39, 40, 41, 48–9,
    69, 87, 101, 103, 105, 114–15, 119
Petrarchism 31, 35, 36, 105, 106
Piccoli maestri, I 78
Piccolo mondo antico 98
Piccolomini, Enea Silvio 88, 119
Piedmont-Savoy 10
Pier delle Vigne 87
Pirandello, Luigi, 15, 42, 48, 50,
    52–4, 85–6, 95, 119
Pisa 68

Pisana, La 74
Platonic Academy 47
Platonism 88
poesia 37, 42
poesia giocosa 35–6
Poliziano, Angelo 89, 119
Popes, *see* Papacy
Principe, Il 70–1
Promessi sposi, I 12, 40–2, 72–4
Prose della volgar lingua 30
Proust, Marcel 110
Provençal 27, 29
psychoanalysis 83, 85
Purgatorio 66, 68, 99–100
purism 33

Q

questione della lingua 12, 31

R

Ravenna 102
readers and reading 34–5, 40, 43,
    45, 48, 72, 81, 83, 85, 98, 100,
    103, 104, 109, 110, 112
realism 2, 15, 41, 53, 54, 55, 61,
    83, 101
Recanati 33
Renaissance 2, 5, 9, 10, 13, 35, 48,
    80, 104, 108, 114
Renzo 73
repubblichini 18
republicanism 11, 60, 62, 69, 71
*Rerum vulgarium fragmenta, see
    Canzoniere, Il*
Resistance 17, 60, 63, 76, 77, 110
Restoration 73
rhetoric 12, 25, 41, 69, 74, 110
rhyme 23, 28
Rinaldo 45
Risorgimento 2, 11, 13, 16, 40, 71,
    73, 80, 86
Robert of Anjou 101
Romana, La 95

romance 91, 101
Romanticism 14, 24, 33–5, 48, 49, 50, 71–2, 86, 97
romanzi d'appendice 109
Rome 10, 11, 13, 14, 28, 42, 67, 96, 97
Roselli, Amelia 112, 119
Rossellini, Roberto 55
Rossetti, Christina 110
Ruggiero 91–4

S

Salò 18, 63
Sanguineti, Edoardo 37, 38, 119
Sannazaro, Iacopo, 119
Santo, Il 98
Sardinia 1, 109
Sarpi, Paolo 71, 119
satire 36, 71, 102
Satura 39
Saviano, Roberto 79, 119
Schmitz, Ettore, *see* Svevo, Italo
Sciascia, Leonardo, 78, 96, 119
Scienza nova, La 95
Scotland 1
scriptures 86
secularism 80, 81–98
Sei personaggi in cerca d'autore 53–4
semiotics 57–8, 78
Sempione strizza l'occhio al Fréjus, Il 68
Seneca 28
Sentiero dei nidi di ragno, Il 77
Sentimento del tempo, Il 25
Se questo è un uomo 96
Sereni, Vittorio 78
Servitore di due padroni, Il 49
Shakespeare 101
Sicily 1, 10, 14, 16, 30, 42, 61–3, 74, 78
Siena 35
signorie 9, 80
Silone, Ignazio 12, 76, 119

Silvestro 61–3, 64
Simonetta Vespucci 89
simoniacs 67
Sior Todero brontolon 49
socialists and socialism 5–6, 16, 18, 19, 74, 75, 85, 98
Sofronia 45
Song of Roland 90
sonnet 30, 36, 114
Sostiene Pereira 79
South 10, 14, 15, 19, 76–7
Spanish Civil War 60, 62
Spain 10, 41, 73
sprezzatura 90
Stampa, Gaspara 106, 119
Stanze per la giostra 89
studia humanitatis 88, 90
style 27, 28, 29, 31, 32, 35, 36, 39, 41, 43, 44–8, 55, 69, 74, 75, 111
Svevo, Italo 12, 42–3, 81–6, 94, 95, 116, 119
Switzerland 1, 76

T

Tabucchi, Antonio 79, 119
Tancredi 45
Tarabotti, Arcangela 109, 119
Tasso, Torquato 9, 36, 44–8, 94, 115, 119
Teatro comico, Il 49
television 13
terza rima 36, 106
Teseida, La 101
theatre 49, 50, 54, 79
theory 20, 43, 44–59
Togliatti, Palmiro 64
Torelli family 9
totalitarianism 16
tradition 3, 14, 16, 20, 21, 22–43, 95, 110
tragedy 40
translations 64, 76, 103
tre corone (three crowns) 2, 11
Trieste 12, 81

Index

Triumphi 28
troubadours 29
Turin 14, 55, 76, 110
Tuscany and Tuscan 10, 12, 27, 32

U

Udine 23
Ultime lettere di Jacopo Ortis, Le 72
Ugolino 87
Ulysses 87
Umorismo, L' 52–3
Ungaretti, Giuseppe 22–6, 36, 38, 39, 119
Una donna 110
Unification 2, 10, 11, 13, 15, 74, 80, 97
universities 58
Uomini e no 63
Uomo che guarda, L' 96
Urbino 89

V

Valduga, Patrizia 112, 120
Valéry, Paul 26
Vatican, *see* Papacy
Veneto 11, 73
Venice 9, 10, 49, 72, 73, 106, 108

Verga, Giovanni 2, 15, 42, 74–6, 86, 116, 120
Vergerio, Pierpaolo 88, 120
verismo 74
vernacular (*volgare*) 2, 30, 105
Viaggio a Roma, Il 96
Vico, Giambattista 95, 120
Victor Emanuel II 11
Villeggiatura trilogy 49
Virgil 27, 65–6, 100
virtù 71
Visconte dimezzato, Il 77
Visconti family 69
Visconti, Luchino 55
Vita nova 27, 29, 47
Vittorini, Elio 55, 60–4, 76, 78, 116, 120

W

Woolf, Virginia 109
Wordsworth, William 24
World War I 22, 81, 83, 95
World War II 10, 14, 15, 16, 19, 39, 42, 57, 96

Z

Zanzotto, Andrea 22, 37, 120
Zibaldone 50
Zola, Émile 74

ENGLISH LITERATURE
A Very Short Introduction
Jonathan Bate

Sweeping across two millennia and every literary genre, acclaimed scholar and biographer Jonathan Bate provides a dazzling introduction to English Literature. The focus is wide, shifting from the birth of the novel and the brilliance of English comedy to the deep Englishness of landscape poetry and the ethnic diversity of Britain's Nobel literature laureates. It goes on to provide a more in-depth analysis, with close readings from an extraordinary scene in King Lear to a war poem by Carol Ann Duffy, and a series of striking examples of how literary texts change as they are transmitted from writer to reader.

www.oup.com/vsi

GERMAN LITERATURE
A Very Short Introduction
Nicholas Boyle

German writers, from Luther and Goethe to Heine, Brecht, and Günter Grass, have had a profound influence on the modern world. This *Very Short Introduction* presents an engrossing tour of the course of German literature from the late Middle Ages to the present, focussing especially on the last 250 years. Emphasizing the economic and religious context of many masterpieces of German literature, it highlights how they can be interpreted as responses to social and political changes within an often violent and tragic history. The result is a new and clear perspective which illuminates the power of German literature and the German intellectual tradition, and its impact on the wider cultural world.

> 'Boyle has a sure touch and an obvious authority...this is a balanced and lively introduction to German literature.'
>
> **Ben Hutchinson, TLS**